GONEVILLE

WINNER OF ADAM FOUNDATION PRIZE IN CREATIVE WRITING

LONGLISTED FOR ROYAL SOCIETY TE APĀRANGI AWARD
FOR GENERAL NON-FICTION

'Enter this memoir and you enter the joy of language, the joy of music, the hurdy-gurdy of young life … I seriously hope to read another book penned by Bollinger, he is so very, very good'
PAULA GREEN, *The Sunday Star-Times*

'Stunning ... As with Dylan's *Chronicles* or Patti Smith's *Just Kids* [a book] to return to, re-read and then re-read again'
SIMON SWEETMAN, *Off the Tracks*

'A teenager with the music bug and the freedom to roam discovers an alternative society, of rebels and refugees, musos and marijuana'
CHRIS BOURKE, author of *Blue Smoke*

'A superb book … this is very fine journalism, dressed-down but dapper. Bollinger's prose is crisp as a freshly ironed shirt, the fabric is colourful without being flashy, the cut is immaculate, the top-stitching stylishly understated, all excess adornment stripped away so that what remains really shines'
GRANT SMITHIES, *Fairfax Media*

'No stone (or stoner) unturned … New Zealand music history at its finest'
KARYN HAY, *RadioLIVE*

'Bollinger is that rare writer on music … he's a musician himself and understands what is actually taking place when he writes about it … In one bravura section, he sets himself the challenge of conveying in words the experience of hearing a performance by Mammal that no one is ever likely to hear. He succeeds brilliantly'
PAUL LITTLE, *North & South*

'Bollinger claims he didn't set out to write a memoir, but some of the book's crispest, most evocative writing is about personal moments'
JAMES BELFIELD, *New Zealand Listener*

'A great read'
MEL HOMER and MIKE PURU, *The Café*, TV3

Also by Nick Bollinger

How to Listen to Pop Music
100 Essential New Zealand Albums

GONEVILLE

NICK BOLLINGER

a memoir

First edition published in 2016 by Awa Press,
Unit 1, Level 3, 11 Vivian Street, Wellington 6011, New Zealand.

First reprinted 2017.

ISBN 978-1-927249-54-3

Ebook formats
Epub 978-1-927249-55-0
Mobi 978-1-927249-56-7

A catalogue record for this book is available from the National Library of New Zealand.

Front cover: Rough Justice on their first trip to Auckland, 1977. From left: Stephen Jessup, Peter Kennedy, Rick Bryant, Simon Page, Nick Bollinger and Martin Highland: photograph by Murray Cammick

Back cover: Rick Bryant, Martin Highland and Nick Bollinger, the Island of Real Café, Auckland, 1978: photograph by Murray Cammick

Author photo: Katherine McRae

Cover designed by Pieta Brenton, pietabrenton.com
Typesetting by Tina Delceg
This book is typeset in Fournier
Printed by 1010 Printing Asia Ltd

Find more great books at awapress.com

Produced with the assistance of

creative nz
ARTS COUNCIL OF NEW ZEALAND TOI AOTEAROA

For Rick

CONTENTS

PREFACE

This book is not a history, although I uncover some history in the telling. While much of it concerns music, I would hesitate to call it musicology. Nor have I set out to write a memoir, although the story starts in the memory. I am writing to make better sense of some things I saw and heard when I was young, the kind of things that determine what you do with the rest of your life.

Growing up in Wellington, I was a busy kid. I swung on vines and built forts in the Town Belt, printed my own newspapers and handed them out in the school playground, saved up to buy the latest Beatles' singles, and made up songs. Yet by the time I reached my teens I was in a liminal zone. It was as though a world existed behind the one I was living in, a world I was catching glimpses of – as you do when someone opens a door to a room you want to enter and explore, yet the door swings shut before you get there. This was the world the music came from, and maybe other things even more important. I felt that if I could just gain access to this world all its mysteries would be explained and my real life would begin.

But there was another world too, one that was in many ways even more remote, although I walked through it every day. This was the world where most New Zealand males seemed to feel at home. It was a place where rugby mattered more than music, where drinking beer was the only acceptable way of altering your consciousness, and old men in suits were entrusted with the interests of the nation. Women were left on the margins. This view was reinforced by newspapers, politicians, school principals, and other figures of power and authority.

I knew I didn't belong to that world, yet I sensed I would somehow need to navigate a path through it, defend myself against it, perhaps even challenge it. It wasn't until many years later that I began to understand that music had a story to tell about these two versions of New Zealand, and that by listening to it, and paying attention to some of the people who created it or gave it a space in which to exist, I could learn something more about the country I lived in.

Essentially, this book encapsulates a decade. I'll call it the '70s, although for me the decade begins in 1971 – the year I turned thirteen, started college, and began to get glimpses through that mystery door – and ends in 1981, the year of the Springbok tour, when New Zealand's two worlds came into violent collision. Inevitably, the story extends either side of this time frame. The '60s – a decade that New Zealand really experienced in the '70s, as Tim Finn once said to me in an interview – were formative, for me and the characters in this story. Other events have their beginnings in the '50s and even earlier. And looking back now, after more than forty years, many insights have been informed by the time that has passed in between.

There were a lot of New Zealanders who did important things in music during this period. Not all of them will appear in these pages. The starting point for this story is simply the music that mattered to me. Some of it became popular but much still remains obscure. One reason for writing is to shine a light on some of that lost or forgotten music. Among the people who made it were a few I got to know well. In particular there's Rick Bryant, a citizen, if ever I met one, of that other New Zealand, the world behind the door. Other people in these pages I had never spoken to before my need to understand something about my own experience led me to seek them out.

Perhaps as significant as the musicians are two entrepreneurs. In the early '70s, Graeme Nesbitt and Richard Holden were both active and creative in delivering music to local audiences. They weren't the only ones, but it would be hard to find any who possessed more singular or contrasting visions of what New Zealand's music scene could or should be.

The other person in this story is me. I am a reluctant character. I have tried on a number of occasions to make myself invisible or to exit these pages altogether, and in a few places I have just about succeeded. Yet, in the end, the obsessions, digressions and confessions you'll find here – and many of the stories – are mine.

And Goneville? It is a name that kept coming up as I was writing this book, and each time its meaning shifted a little. It's almost Gonville, the suburb of Whanganui where Johnny Devlin, New Zealand's first rock 'n' roll star, grew up, so arguably the birthplace of New Zealand rock 'n' roll. But it is also an imaginary place that might be every obscure New Zealand town that every obscure New Zealand band ever played. Rough Justice, a band you will read about in this book, played in many Gonevilles. It is, too, a name for the past: that other country to which you can never return. It has a touch of the hipster vernacular, the sort of word I imagine the early pot smokers might have used to describe their state of mind. It also turns up in a song by Tony Backhouse that Rough Justice used to play – 'maybe the Goneville line is down'.

It's a place you could almost find on a map, but not quite.

01
THE RICK BRYANT SCHOOL OF ROCK 'N' ROLL

Wellington, April 1977. The cottage perches on the side of a steep hill in the shadow of the Chinese embassy. Flakes of pale paint hang from the weatherboards. I've climbed the zigzag path and crooked wooden stairs and now stand on the veranda under a rusted corrugated-iron awning. Below me on the narrow road are Jaguars, early 1950s models, going nowhere. One has a flat tyre. Another has a window missing and a brick wedged hard against the front wheel. And there is yet another up the street, a maroon Mark VII, its nose just visible around the sharp bend. Once, outside a concert at Downstage Theatre, I saw the man who has summoned me here drive slowly past in this car with a police car on his tail.

And on the road, occupying the space of three cars, is the bus, an ex-Railways Bedford with patches of the original lime green showing through its unfinished repaint. It has been decorated with Renaissance cherubs, slightly grazed, as though they may have flown too close to the ground. Above the windscreen the destination sign reads ROCK 'N' ROLL. On the long panel down one side, in bold baroque capitals, are the words ROUGH JUSTICE.

I knock and the door opens. The woman is in her early twenties, perhaps two or three years older than me, with fair hair and a wide smile. 'You must be Nick. I'm Janet.' This is Janet Clouston, who has phoned the day before to say that Rick Bryant has requested a visit. The call was unexpected: I don't really know Rick, although I know a lot of stories about him. It feels as though this is becoming one of them.

Janet leads me through a dark hallway into a sitting room lined from floor to ceiling with books. It's like an antiquarian's storeroom. I see Shakespeare and Proust and Beckett and a history of the opium trade. The only collection this size I've ever seen is my father's. A bright poster on a wall proclaims: A ROCK BAND ON TOUR – BETTER CALL GROUND CONTROL. Arranged on a sideboard is a collection of ceramic plates bearing images of crayfish. I don't see Rick but, like the telltale scent when you enter a creature's lair, the earthy smell of pot tells me he is home. Then, through a doorway to another room, I notice him, flat on a bed, his head wreathed in smoke.

Removing the joint from his mouth, Rick beckons me, thanks me for coming, winces with pain, and motions me to take a seat. Between drags he explains that he has hurt his fucking back making repairs to the bus but expects to be on his feet again in a few days. His band, Rough Justice, which he formed after his release from prison last year, has broken up. Three members handed in their notice mid-tour, so he left them on the roadside somewhere in the central North Island and drove off.

He pauses, gazes into the middle distance, and releases a long loud staccato laugh as he recalls the mutineers' misjudgement, then curses at the effect laughter has on his herniated disc. He's starting a new band, he says, and he's keeping the name Rough Justice. After all, it's his fucking name, isn't it? And anyway Janet has already painted it on the bus. He has two musicians signed up. Would I consider being the third?

I have been listening to Rick sing since I was thirteen. Now, seated at his bedside as he outlines his proposal, I feel as though I'm being asked to become a character in a book that, until this moment, might have been a work of fiction. I am eighteen. In the two years since I left school I have stayed up all night, slept all day, practised my bass playing, fallen hopelessly in love, and performed occasionally with a group called The Windy City Strugglers. I have been fired from building sites, failed as a furniture mover, and almost succeeded as a cellarman until I lost control of a booze-stacked trolley and flooded the kitchen of the Commercial Travellers' Club. A couple of months ago I enrolled at university, acting on the advice I imagine my father would have given me. 'A bright bugger like you might have more fun doing a few papers than mopping up after a bunch of alcoholic salesmen,' I could hear him say. But joining a full-time band sounded even better. And there was no one to tell me not to.

I'm not sure I'm good enough to play in Rick's band. I am in awe of all the different bass players I have seen in his various bands – Steve Hemmens, Patrick Bleakley, and particularly Mark Hornibrook – but could there be a better way to learn? Rick asks what I'm studying, tells me an intelligent person who has grown up around books doesn't need to go to university, wonders if I realise that Captain Beefheart ripped it all off Howlin' Wolf, and by the way have I read any Evelyn Waugh?

He says he has some business to attend to. It's not clear what the nature of this business is, but he seems to be able to conduct it by telephone from his current prone position, and suggests I adjourn to the sitting room where there is a good stereo and help myself to a glass of wine.

He has albums I've never seen by names I've come to know as standard-bearers of soul music – James Brown, Aretha Franklin, Bobby 'Blue' Bland – and others I've never heard of – Rasputin's Stash, Ten Wheel Drive, Harold Melvin & The Blue Notes. 'Let me know if you hear anything you think we could learn,' Rick calls from the other room. Aretha is singing 'Baby I Love You', I'm sipping from a jar of something plum-coloured and soul-warming, and my brief university career has just come to an end.

02
MESMERISING ECHOES

Wellington Station was shaking like the inside of a speaker box. I was twelve, in my last year of primary school, and had signed up, with my brother, to play a small part in a children's television serial about a group of schoolkids who catch a bank robber. The director, Derek Morton, was a friend of our older cousin Alun Bollinger, which is how two kids like us, with no experience in acting or television, came to be involved. Derek also knew the filmmaker, Geoff Murphy, who had come up with the story, and Bruno Lawrence, a drummer and actor who was playing one of the robbers.

I was more interested in music than movie-making. The Beatles had been my obsession since a Christmas several years before, when Alun and his sister Sue had played me some of their new records. Nothing before had ever made me feel as good as the shot of rhythm and noise that was 'Twist and Shout'. From that day on I sought out The Beatles everywhere. I listened to the *Sunset Show*, five p.m. every weekday on Radio 2ZB, where their songs would be sandwiched between miserably slow stuff such

as Andy Williams singing 'On the Street Where You Live' and tunes I liked almost as much as The Beatles', like Manfred Mann's 'Do Wah Diddy Diddy' and The Supremes' 'Baby Love'. But The Beatles had my loyalty. I saved my pocket money, one shilling a week, until I had enough to buy my own 45 of 'Twist and Shout', followed by others: 'Can't Buy Me Love', 'A Hard Day's Night', 'I Feel Fine', 'Ticket To Ride'.

When The Beatles came to New Zealand I failed to persuade my parents to let me go and see them. After all, I had just turned six. But Dad agreed to take me to *A Hard Day's Night*. It was a matinee and the theatre was half empty, but sitting in the front row were two girls who screamed and sobbed throughout the film.

Over the next few years The Beatles would change in fascinating and unpredictable ways. 'Strawberry Fields Forever'. 'I Am the Walrus'. 'Revolution'. Their records taught me to listen, and I would willingly receive any new combination of sounds they threw at me. When my father read me a newspaper story about the band bringing London traffic to a halt by playing a concert on a rooftop, I persuaded my brother and a couple of friends after school to climb on to the roof of the Cable Car station, where I shouted Beatles' songs until the authorities ordered us down.

I augmented my collection of singles with LPs I'd get for Christmas or birthdays if I was lucky. But I could never afford all the music I wanted, so I was looking forward to the money I'd earn from the television programme. It took up more time than I expected. What was initially proposed as three weeks' work, mostly during school holidays, dragged on for half the year. We would regularly find Derek waiting for us at the school gate at three o'clock, ready to whisk us to Newtown where, in those pre-health-and-safety days, he would have us scaling walls, jumping off roofs, running up and down stairwells chased by a fat man dressed as a policeman, and wielding samurai swords in vacant lots, while he tried to get as much footage as he could before the light died.

Derek was ginger-bearded and curly-haired and wore orange and black striped trousers. He wasn't a hippie exactly: he was a bit older than the longhaired grown-ups I'd started to see around town, who all looked like they might be in rock groups. I remembered a phrase I'd heard Dad use once: 'carnival anarchist'.

A man called Bill Dwyer had come to one of the political meetings my parents sometimes held in our living room and left behind his hat, a green felt object with a greasy stain on the brim. Bill Dwyer didn't come back for his hat. My parents didn't take the hat back to Bill Dwyer. Tim and I took to wearing it in our games of dress-ups. It became known as Bill Dwyer's Hat.

One day I heard Mum and Dad talking about Bill Dwyer. It was the first time I'd heard the name without mention of his hat. The conversation was full of words I didn't know: 'arrested', 'convicted', 'deported'.

'Who is Bill Dwyer?' I asked.

'He's a carnival anarchist,' Dad said. I had no idea what a carnival anarchist was but I liked the way it sounded. Perhaps Derek was a carnival anarchist too? He would laugh like a lunatic when something went right – for example, the paint bomb aimed at the clothesline hit its target first time – and even more maniacally when something went wrong, like the time the steering wheel came off in Bruno's hands as a bunch of us kids dragged him from the getaway car. He also taught us fantastic swear words, and rude things to say like, 'We're not here to fuck spiders.' But after a few months the novelty started to wear off.

One Saturday Derek turned up to collect us from our homes at about seven o'clock in the morning. Before we went to Newtown to get started on the day's perilous activities, he had to make a couple of stops. We went to a house in Webb Street where we picked up Bruno, then headed to the Railway Station. Derek

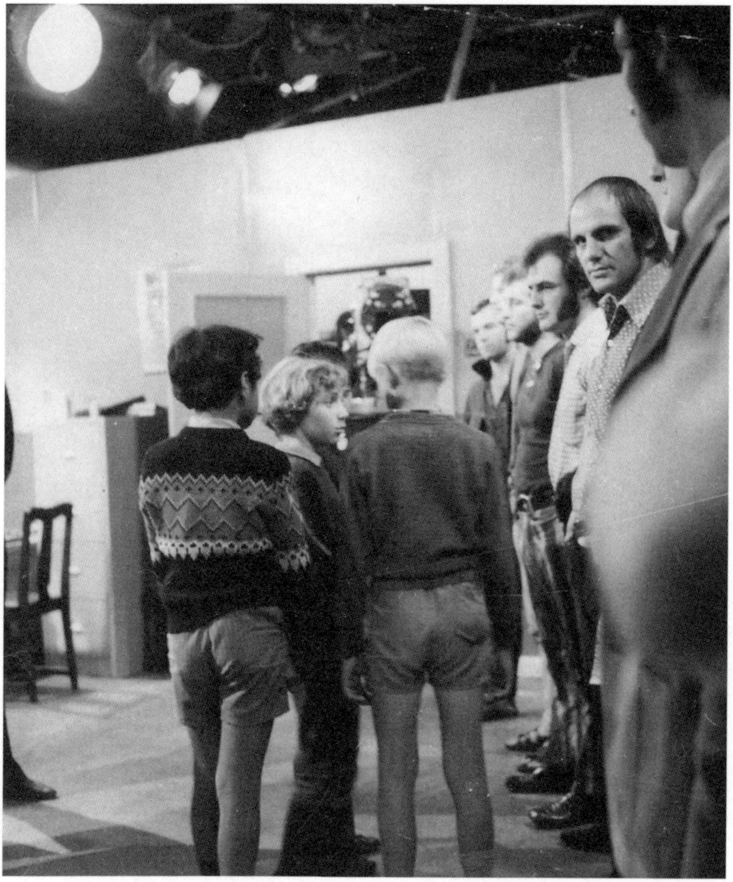

explained that it was the start of the University Arts Festival, although I wasn't sure what that meant.

As we got out of the car in front of the station's grand sandstone entrance, with its eight towering pillars and Roman-numeralled clock, I could hear a fantastic noise. Just inside, by the statue of Kupe, a band was playing. A colourfully dishevelled crowd was gathered around them. A few people were twirling about, arms out, eyes closed, hair flicking across their faces.

'Well, are you gonna dance?' Bruno said, as though surprised Tim and I weren't rushing to join in. No, I wasn't going to dance. I just stood there amazed by the sound, the way it seemed to be moving around so much inside the huge high chamber of the station's foyer. I couldn't hear where the notes began, only their mesmerising echoes.

I'd seen a live band once before, when The Fourmyula had played on a summer night in the Botanic Garden near our house. Then I had recognised songs from the radio, but the music this band was making was louder and stranger and I knew none of the songs. Derek said the band was called Simon and The Mammals.

After a while Bruno went off to talk to the musicians and Derek took us to a platform where students were arriving from Auckland. They stumbled out of the carriages, longhaired teenagers, some with bare feet, some carrying sleeping bags. As they moved towards the foyer someone stretched a length of ribbon across the entrance, a man with a beard, beret and pair of scissors stepped forward and cut it, and the whole group cheered.

03
REBELS AND REFUGEES

It is my first year at Onslow College in the wind-shocked suburb of Johnsonville. In a railway carriage full of boys and girls from the city's western suburbs – Kelburn, Karori, Northland, Wadestown – I make the daily journey seven kilometres north to the newest state secondary school in the region. The other colleges around Wellington have all existed in one form or another since the nineteenth century but Onslow opened only in the 1950s, in time to cater for the post-war baby boom. To our parents – Pākehā, middle-class, many of them public servants, some teachers themselves – it is the school most likely to provide the modern, enlightened education they envision for us. To me, it seems the school where I will find the fewest obstacles to the adventures I am determined to have.

As we straggle through Wellington Railway Station to catch the Johnsonville unit other teenagers pass us going in the opposite direction: commuters from the northern suburbs heading to the traditional single-sex institutions – Wellington College and Wellington Girls' College. I feel superior, slightly sorry for the boys with their compulsory caps and short-back-and-sides haircuts and the girls in their shapeless smocks.

On board we squeeze into facing seats. My bare knees bunch up against those of the fellow first-year sitting opposite. The train clatters north away from the city and the harbour, over the bridge at Ngauranga, through short tunnels, past the state houses of Ngaio and lush gardens of Khandallah, towards the new subdivisions of Johnsonville.

A poster above the window declares it is compulsory for every New Zealand male to enrol for military training by the age of twenty. Ballots based on birth dates will then be conducted. This means some of the boys in this carriage who will be leaving school at the end of the year will later go, against their will, into the army. Well, they're not going to make me do that. New Zealand has troops in Vietnam, fighting a war that's nothing to do with me. I've joined OHMS, Organisation to Halt Military Service. I have the badge pinned to the canvas army surplus bag I use to carry my schoolbooks and I've been on marches, mobilisations as they're called.

I've also mobilised against The Bomb. The Americans and Russians want to blow each other up and take the rest of the world with them, and now the French have nuclear weapons and are testing them in the South Pacific. And then there is The Tour. Last year there were protests to try to stop the All Blacks going to play rugby against the Springboks in South Africa. They have apartheid over there, which means black people don't have rights. They're not even allowed to vote. HART, that's Halt All Racist Tours, reckons the only way to make those white South Africans change is to take away the things they love, like rugby.

A guy called Tim Shadbolt got arrested running on to the tarmac at Wellington Airport, trying to stop the All Blacks' plane from taking off.

The New Zealand government won't stop the war, the bomb or the tour. The prime minister, Keith Holyoake, has been in parliament since 1932. Everything about him – his short hair, his suit, his pompous voice – belongs to the past. I bet he hasn't even heard The Beatles. And then there's Muldoon. The Pig, we call him. He's minister of finance but people say he'll take over from Holyoake in the end and that will be even worse.

Back then, my way of expressing dissent was refusing to cut my hair. I looked like a haystack with a pair of arms poking out. These were usually wrapped around a couple of LPs. After school and on weekends I'd wear a combination of torn jeans, an outsized seaman's jersey and a poncho purloined from my mother's wardrobe. From mid-autumn I usually had an oilskin parka over the top, which I kept on all day. At school I dressed in whatever variations on the school uniform I could get away with. For a while I wore a pink tie-dyed T-shirt underneath my regulation grey long-sleeved one, until my maths teacher, Miss Barnes, who was also a Sunday school instructor, caught a flash of colour and sent me to the Glass Box, a holding pen outside the principal's office, where miscreants went to await sentencing.

The Glass Box was a good place to make friends. That's where I met Bruce. He was a few years ahead of me, one of the few senior students who could be bothered talking to juniors. He wore love beads, kept his shirt untucked, and asked me what music I'd been listening to. Although obviously smart, he had failed School C so was repeating his fifth form year; he seemed to have his own seat in the box.

One day another student popped his head around the side and told us about a guerrilla theatre event being planned for school assembly the following Monday. On a given cue, rebel students would storm the stage. The student representative, who was in on the plot, would be symbolically slain and carried from the hall draped in a flag, while someone else rushed down the aisle throwing hand-rolled raspberry-leaf cigarettes into the crowd. Would I participate, perhaps be one of the pallbearers? Fuck, yeah!

As much as I fancied myself as a teenage rebel taking a stand against a world of crazy rules and warmongers, the truth was that the principles I stood for had for the most part been formed, fought for and handed on to me by my family. I would have shown more independent thinking if I'd I cut my hair and joined the Young Nats.

My mother, Marei, had stepped off the boat in Wellington in 1939, a bright bewildered three-year-old who could understand and speak some German but not a word of English. She had just escaped from Hitler. With her were her mother, father, six-year-old brother and an elderly woman dressed entirely in black and known as Loelein.

My mother's mother, Maria, had grown up in Berlin, the youngest child and only daughter of an intellectual Jewish family. Loelein had been Maria's governess. Maria became a successful actress, playing classical roles in Germany's major theatres. When the revered poet Rainer Maria Rilke died, she was asked

to read at his memorial. In 1931, she married a German Catholic magistrate and moved to Hamburg. Loelein went with her.

A little later the trio moved to Cologne, where my mother and her brother were born. In 1938, as the Jewish persecution intensified, Maria left for England, pretending she was going on holiday. She would not return to Germany. After several months Loelein followed, bringing the children with her. They had nothing with them but a few clothes and some money Loelein had hidden between the pages of a photograph album. Eventually my grandfather left Germany as well. The family took shelter in a convent in Newcastle until 1939, when they were granted visas to emigrate to New Zealand just before the outbreak of war.

Despite being Jewish refugees, once in New Zealand the German nationals were treated with suspicion. As 'enemy aliens' they were required to report regularly to the police, especially whenever they planned to venture outside Wellington. This compounded their strong sense of being different in a country where simple things like coffee beans and pumpernickel bread were considered exotic, and recreation meant watching rugby, not reading Rilke.

They met others suffering from similar cultural dislocation, among them Harry Seresin, a Jewish refugee from Russia who had arrived the same year and would start Wellington's first European-style coffee shop, as well as its first professional theatre. A visitor to the Seresins remembers Harry shaking his head and muttering, as he picked up a broken beer bottle someone had left on his front lawn, 'Ah, the New Zealand national sport.'

My grandfather was forbidden by war regulations from practising in the legal profession. He took a job as a double bass player in a dance band. His training had been strictly classical, and it had never been his ambition to play professionally: mastering an instrument had simply been part of his broad education as a cultured young German. The other musicians in the band were not unfriendly, although they laughed at his inability to play the simple popular songs of the day without a notated score. When he told them his name – Adolf Dronke – they shook their heads and grimaced. He became John.

But my grandparents also made many friends, especially among poets, actors, painters and composers, New Zealanders who, even though born in the country, shared some of their estrangement from the prevailing culture. My grandmother Maria began teaching speech and drama and giving poetry recitals; by the 1950s she had begun to include the works of new friends such as Denis Glover and James K. Baxter alongside those of European poets. The artist Colin McCahon did a lighting design for her production of Ibsen's *The Master Builder*, and she collaborated with composer Douglas Lilburn on settings of Rilke. John became a founding member of the National Orchestra. This was the environment in which my mother grew up: the arts were the essence of life, and the world could be divided into those who were for you and those who were against.

My father, Conrad Bollinger, who was always known as Con, was already a rebel by the time he met the teenage Marei in the mid 1950s. His father had died before he was born; he and his elder brother and sister had been raised by his mother and a large assortment of aunts who lived near the family's Khandallah home. Surrounded by books and strong intelligent women, he immersed himself in history and literature and began to develop a world view based on humanist ideals. The journal he kept in 1946, the year he turned seventeen, begins with quotes, copied by hand, from John Stuart Mill, Albert Einstein and George Loveless of the Tolpuddle Martyrs. Con came to the attention of the Security Intelligence Service a couple of years later when he placed copies of a pamphlet he had written opposing conscription in the foyer of the local Anglican church. By then he had joined the Communist Party, although he would resign in protest in 1956 after the Soviets invaded Hungary.

In the early 1960s Con became publicist for the New Zealand branch of the Campaign for Nuclear Disarmament and chaired two organisations, the Socialist Forum and the Committee on Vietnam. Through most of the decade he worked for the Public Service Association, the union for the country's civil servants, eventually leaving it to teach English at Victoria University. He was always going to meetings, or hosting political gatherings at our house. Before I could walk I had ridden on his shoulders on CND marches. I grew up in a household where war and apartheid were condemned, Holyoake was an American puppet, and Bill Dwyer's hat hung in the hall.

An older cousin recently told me of an occasion, before I was born, when my father had taken him to watch a rugby game at Athletic Park. Footing it home afterwards, Con had said they could walk down the middle of street if they wanted to because they were New Zealanders and the All Blacks had just won a test. From as early as I can remember, though, the national sport was rarely mentioned in our household without some reference to South Africa, and how New Zealand should be boycotting it as long as the racist apartheid system remained. When it was reported in the newspaper that a cricket pitch in Wellington had been attacked with shovels on the eve of a visit by a South African team, my father whispered to me that Mum had driven the getaway car. Dad never learned to drive.

As kids, we were encouraged to ask questions and express opinions. At the big wooden dinner table in our house at Kelburn's North Terrace the atmosphere was egalitarian and loud. I sometimes had arguments with my parents – Dad once stopped me leaving the house before I'd finished my homework by closing the living-room door and gently but securely sitting on me as I kicked and yelled helplessly – but I knew they were really on my side. My schoolmates seemed to like coming around. My father would emerge from his study, or my mother from the garden, to question them about their lives, their families, their dreams. Some, like my friend Dave, would spend hours in conversation with my father. I'm not even sure what they talked about. I began to realise that to most of my friends having an adult treat you as an equal and take an interest in your ideas was unusual.

My father had a certain way of greeting everyone, whether his students, colleagues, family, countless acquaintances or friends of his kids. He would say, 'Are you happy?' then pause long enough for them to consider the question. I'd hear him ask visitors if they were happy before they set foot in the front door, and people we met in the street. For one of his political cobbers the answer might be, 'No, I'm bloody not,' followed by an anti-government diatribe. If it was one of his students, the question could be taken as invitation to confide a problem they were having with an essay,

ESCALATE
THE PEACE
WITHDRAW
FROM VIETNA

a flatmate or a lover. To this day, when I meet people who knew my father they will inevitably tell me: *There's something I always remember about your father. He asked me if I was happy. I really had to think about it. It seemed like he really wanted to know.*

If he asked me, I'd consider my situation, weigh up the things that seemed to be going right against the things that were going wrong and conclude that on balance, yeah, I was happy.

RESISTANCE
BOOKSHOP

04
FELLOW DISSENTERS

From my college timetable it might have looked as though I was studying English, French, maths, science and art, but whichever classes I attended what I was usually thinking about was rock music. Even in a school with Onslow's progressive reputation, that put me in a minority. I felt surrounded by boys who were far more concerned with playing rugby or drinking beer. A few, like me, grew their hair long in rough imitation of a rock star but most still wore it short in the manner of an All Black or an accountant. Some were bullies. There was a hulking stubble-haired fifth-former who could not pass me in the corridor without pausing to grab the front of my jersey, lift me in the air and drop me violently to the ground.

When I met a boy called Martin I recognised him as a fellow dissenter. As a sign of liberalism Onslow had done away with ties, and regulations required male students to wear the top button of our grey shirts undone. Martin always wore his done up. He looked oddly formal. 'It's a statement of my individuality,' was how he explained it to me.

We had become friends during a PE class, jogging around the bottom field. 'I don't mind physical exercise but I have a moral and philosophical objection to competitive sport,' he said as we ran side by side. By the time our circuit of the field was complete he had quoted, from a newspaper clipping he carried in his pocket, the Jewish immigrant and social agitator Dr Erich Geiringer on rugby and the Kiwi male psyche, and we had established a mutual interest in The Beatles.

After that, a small group of us started gathering at Martin's place after school, on weekends or even during class time to pursue our study of a small but growing collection of albums. Peter McLuskie had the first Doors album and *The Who Live At Leeds*. Andy had The Rolling Stones' *Beggars Banquet* and a Folkways record by a blues singer called Blind Snooks Eaglin. Dave had a Mothers of Invention album called *Weasels Ripped My Flesh*. Martin liked The Kinks, which I thought had something to do with the fact his dad came from London. I had my Beatles albums and singles.

We had between us several Jimi Hendrix albums, which we agreed were great, but consensus was not always reached so easily. I recall the gentle music of James Taylor causing an unexpected eruption when Andy, who had bought *Sweet Baby James*, tried to put it on Martin's turntable. Pronouncing it 'wet', Martin wrenched the record from the machine and flung it like a Frisbee across the room.

Occasionally something subterranean would enter our circle, snuck from the collection of an older brother or sister. That was how I first encountered Van Morrison's *Astral Weeks*. With its hushed and unfamiliar sounds – double bass, vibraphone, flute, violins, flamenco guitar – and a voice, which might be in ecstasy or pain, asking me mystifying, mind-tangling questions, the whole album was as magical as it was impenetrable, a glimpse behind a door into an adult world.

It was all boys in our group that first year, partly because none of us were bold enough to ask any girls to join us, or thought any would want to (although we thought a lot about girls), and partly because so many older, more sophisticated boys seemed to have their attention. Sometimes on a Friday night, when the shops stayed open until nine, we would go into town. We didn't have much buying power, just a little pocket money from our parents or cash earned from paper rounds, but we found cheap ways to entertain ourselves.

Between Lambton Quay and Cuba Street there were half a dozen places that sold records – Record Specialists, Kirkcaldies, DIC, Lamphouse, World Records, Vanvi. We'd stop at each one. Kirkcaldies and DIC, both department stores, had listening rooms furnished with chairs and good stereo speakers. These were surely intended for middle-aged aesthetes who might want to compare Kleiber's version of Beethoven's Fifth with Karajan's, but we could usually convince an elderly sales assistant to let us sample something from the bin labelled 'Popular'. We would crowd in, some seated, some sprawled on the floor, close the door and blast the booth with Black Sabbath or The Rolling Stones.

Eventually the assistant would appear around the door and ask if we would be buying the record. It was a signal: our time was up. We would move on to the music stores. One of us would haul a guitar down from a high rack and try out the few chords we knew while the rest huddled around to watch. The staff would tolerate us for a while, but when I found a Hammond organ in Begg's Music Store plugged in and asking to be played, my primitive attempt at boogie-woogie was halted in the middle of a bar, and I found myself grabbed by the collar and carried to the front door of the shop, where the store manager dropped me into the street.

One place no one seemed to mind us hanging around was the Resistance Bookshop. It was on the second floor of an old wooden villa in Willis Street, above The Merchant Adventurers of Narnia, a clothing shop run by longhaired guys in their mid twenties whose girlfriends wore Indian skirts. Resistance Bookshop sold political literature, books by beat poets, radical magazines, *The Whole Earth Catalogue* and golden badges featuring Mao Tse-tung. It was where I first saw *The Little Red Schoolbook*. Written by a pair of Danish schoolteachers, this was like an instruction manual for the kind of teenagers we thought we might be. It informed us that schoolchildren had a right not to be bored by their teachers, LSD trips lasted for eight or nine hours, and girls could masturbate. We learned the book had been banned in Britain and might soon be banned here too, so we consumed its contents with urgency, sitting for hours on the shop's worn-out armchairs, where horsehair tufts poked through the fabric.

Walking home through town we caught glimpses of another, forbidden world. There were pubs like the Royal Oak, the Speakeasy, the Duke of Edinburgh, the Carlton and the Grand, their windows frosted, light and noise blazing from within. On the streets were characters who seemed to come out only after dark: a middle-aged Māori with black slicked-back hair and a blue satin jacket with ELVIS spelt out in sequins on the back; and Carmen, Wellington's famous transvestite, her bouffant wig bedecked with roses, pearl earrings dangling down to her massive bosom, and a retinue of queens trailing in her wake. One night we stood and watched a band playing old rock 'n' roll songs in the foyer of the Roxy Cinema. The bass player wore an expression of bored cool. I was impressed by his technique for checking his wristwatch mid-song without taking his fingers off the fretboard.

In pursuit of further mysteries I became a card-carrying member of the library of the United States of America Information Service. An older student at Onslow had mentioned it had jazz records. I knew hardly anything about jazz but the names Charles Mingus and John Coltrane had been implanted in my mind because of references to them in an anthology of British beat poets called *The Mersey Sound* and I resolved to find out what they sounded like. I knew where to go: the library was housed in the United States Embassy, which I had once stood outside on a mobilisation.

Entering it felt like crossing enemy lines. I reported to a window made of bulletproof glass, where a receptionist asked me over an intercom that crackled like an old 78 record the purpose of my visit. The door beyond was guarded by an expressionless Marine, fully armed.

Finally I was granted entry. The door clicked open, then closed behind me, and I followed directions down a hallway to a room full of books and filing cabinets. I couldn't see any LPs but I discovered a cabinet that contained a series of filing cards with album titles on them. I found a card with the name of a Mingus record and another by Coltrane and reported to the issues desk.

'I'd like to borrow these,' I said, offering the cards.

'Would you? Are you a member?' demanded the stern and terrifying librarian.

I wasn't.

'Name?'

I stammered an answer.

'Max's son or Conrad's?' she fired back.

How did she know my uncle and my father? Did the embassy keep files on them? Did they know I was against The War? Decades later, when a musician friend was telling me about his favourite aunt, it slowly dawned on me that she was the librarian – in reality a theatre-loving left-winger who had known my family through the small, closely woven Wellington arts community. Perhaps she had been keeping an eye on those war-mad Americans.

The Mingus and Coltrane records had somehow infiltrated this bastion of imperialism. They strike me now as a kind of dissident art. The music was complex and challenging and took me years to comprehend. I also collected a tiny number of New Zealand albums. There was Human Instinct's *Stoned Guitar*, featuring the mind-melting guitar of Billy Te Kahika, usually referred to as Billy TK and sometimes the Māori Hendrix. And there was the sole self-titled album of Highway, a band from Wellington. While these records delivered a respectable number of riffs per minute and sounded okay, even after Hendrix or the Stones, part of the attraction was price: they were cheap. Why local records retailed at half the price of international releases no one could adequately explain. There just seemed to be an unwritten law that Billy TK's thunderous riffs and squally solos, although exciting, were only worth half as much as Hendrix's.

Some of our group got hold of instruments and tried to scare music out of them. Andy impressed the rest of us by figuring out the guitar part to the first track off the Highway LP. A guy called Jeff, who had failed University Entrance and was repeating his sixth form year, had a bass guitar but couldn't play it; he used it as a prop for his impressions of a lead guitarist, writhing in a mime of ecstasy on the floor of the maths room. When he lent me his bass for a weekend I managed to master half the riff of The Beatles' 'Day Tripper' and a simple twelve-bar blues.

The so-called blues 'revival' – young white audiences listening for the first time to music that had been popular among black Americans for decades – had just swept through Britain and America. White rock stars such as Eric Clapton and The Rolling Stones, with repertoires drawing heavily on the blues, were a gateway to the original black musicians; the ones still going strong found themselves, for the first time in their long careers, in front of predominantly white audiences.

In the early '70s New Zealand caught the aftershock of that explosion. Suddenly B.B. King, Muddy Waters, Willie Dixon, Chuck Berry, and Sonny Terry and Brownie McGee, names I had heard mentioned mostly as an influence on the white blues stars, came to New Zealand. My Onslow enclave went to the concerts, where we were confronted with a startlingly different culture.

The first bluesman I saw was B.B. King at the Wellington Town Hall. The way he addressed us as 'ladies and gentlemen', the hair that looked as though it had been varnished into place, the matching suits and near military precision of his band, the formality of the show – all of it was a shock. I had seen hippies in a film about the 1969 Woodstock Festival and was imitating them by dressing as scruffily as I could get away with. I had participated in a student stop-work when the principal of Onslow, not as liberal-minded as our parents and some of our teachers, had ordered us to cut our hair. I was anti-authoritarian on principle. Yet here I was in the presence of a strict disciplinarian. In fact B.B. King's performance had aspects of a school assembly, albeit one where the principal dealt in sexual innuendos and could make his guitar cry like a man in the deepest existential pain. It also had a gravity and dignity beyond anything I had ever witnessed.

British bluesman John Mayall looked more like someone you might see on a mobilisation. With his long hair and headband he could have been a groovy university lecturer, or someone's older brother. He came to New Zealand several years in a row and our gang didn't miss a concert. On one occasion his supporting act was an Auckland group called Split Ends. It seemed an odd choice: the band didn't play blues or anything like it. Yet their music seemed in its own way as exotic as Mayall's. It was certainly unlike anything on the radio at the time. Their songs alternately resembled vaudeville, Elizabethan classical, English folk music and occasionally – just a few bars here and there – pop songs.

Around this time we went to the concert chamber in the Town Hall to see a group called Blerta. We had seen their painted bus around town, and posters announcing: BLERTA IS COMING! Blerta wasn't as much a band as a challenge to the accepted order. Musicians would wander on and off the stage so it was hard to tell how many people were in the group. Some were hairy young rockers with the regulation electric guitars. Others looked older and played what I thought of as jazz instruments – trumpet, saxophone and trombone. Seated at an electric piano, his eyes fixed on some point beyond the chamber's walls, was Chris Seresin, a musician who looked only a only few years older than us yet commanded the keys with a startling intensity. The singer, Corben Simpson, had a voice that soared into the highest corners of the chamber's vaulted ceilings. For the first part of the show he played a bass guitar but by the end he was dancing around the stage, his arms waving like a windmill.

The group combined catchy songs and long lyrical solos with instrumental jams that spiralled into chaos. Black and white Keystone Cops-style scenarios, filmed in recognisable locations around Wellington, played on a screen above the musicians. The films were silent but Ian Watkin, a bearded big-bellied man with a booming voice, stood among the band and improvised a narration. Sometimes one of the actors would wander on to the stage as though he had just stepped out of the screen.

At the centre of it all, behind a set of drums, sat Bruno Lawrence. I already knew who he was. Now, seeing him on stage, I realised why some people thought he was the best drummer in the country. He was the engine that powered the whole sound and determined when the music would change gear, shift into reverse, overtake, or leave the ground.

Bruno's drums always seemed to be falling to bits. Even as he played he would be tightening lugs, repairing stands and reattaching cymbals, yet the rhythm never faltered. It pumped on through everything that happened, whether someone taking a saxophone solo, an actor attempting a tightrope walk, or images flickering on the screen. Dark-eyed, with what remained of his thinning hair flapping about the sides of his face, Bruno seemed both utterly absorbed in his own playing and acutely aware of everything else that was going on. He was older than the others and clearly the leader. During the songs he would often appear to be issuing instructions. Sometimes he would hurl a drumstick at one of the members of the band. But he'd never drop a beat.

There were a few musical events we would not have been seen dead at. 'THE GREATEST TEENAGE NIGHT OF THE YEAR!' proclaimed an *Evening Post* ad for Creation, 1972 winners of the Golden Disc Award, playing at The Sheridan nightclub. The word 'teenage' was the first deterrent. Nor would we have been found at Oodles Coffee Shop where, ads promised, 'Wayne Finch will be singing *middle of the road* music.'

Occasionally, if a band sounded promising and there was no cover charge, we would venture to a café or restaurant that was advertising live music. At The Settlement, a continental-style café run by Harry Seresin, who was the father of Blerta's Chris Seresin, we made two cups of percolated coffee last the length of three sets while we earnestly studied a band known as Olibet. The musicians looked uncomfortable at being closely scrutinised by a tableful of serious schoolboys while the winers and diners were taking little notice.

05
THE UNION HALL

It was Peter McLuskie who knew there was something happening at the university's Union Hall and suggested we go along one Friday night. I wasn't sure they'd let us in as we were only thirteen but Peter was an imposing presence in a greatcoat he'd found at the Love Shop, an exchange bazaar off Cuba Street, and I slipped through the door in his shadow. Once inside we found ourselves in a tunnel of white sheets lit by ultraviolet lamps that gave our teeth, the whites of our eyes and the dust on our trousers a radioactive glow. We stopped, stared at our hands and the particles of light that seemed to be exploding off the sheets, and laughed.

As we emerged from the tunnel into the main body of the hall a guitarist was playing alone on a balcony. In the darkness I could make out the silhouette of his gangly frame and flowing hair as he strummed a fierce rhythm on a small-bodied acoustic guitar and sang a Chuck Berry blues I recognised. On a stage below the balcony there was a band with a flute player and a drummer with a gigantic afro; the shadow on the white cloth behind him made his hair seem even bigger. The band performed unfamiliar songs and long instrumental jams while liquid blobs of colour bubbled and shapeshifted across their faces and instruments. Across a wall of the room and part of the ceiling, more colours were bursting like bombshells. Another wall appeared to be crawling with giant insects. This must be what tripping is like, I thought. There was no alcohol on sale and I don't recall any drinking, but the sweet scent I remember drifting my way must have been marijuana.

When the music was over we followed the crowd to the adjacent Memorial Theatre, where a flickering assortment of music film clips issued from a faltering 16-mm projector. After midnight we stepped, saucer-eyed, back into the suburban night.

After that the Union Hall became a regular destination. I would keep an eye out for notices in *Salient*, the student newspaper my father brought home from the university. The events were supposed to be restricted to university students but no one ever asked for ID. The doors would open around eight at night but the music didn't start until nine. Early comers would either mingle in the shadows or, like me, sit up close to the stage on the hard linoleum floor waiting for something to happen. Determined not to miss anything, I would often be there in time to catch the bands sound-checking. One night I watched in fascination as a musician I later came to know as Simon Morris tuned every instrument on the stage.

Once the show got underway people would get up and dance, sometimes in couples but often in the solo freestyle mode I'd observed in the Woodstock film. I'd maintain my cross-legged position on the ground until it became untenable, then go looking for an alternative vantage point. One night I found a small platform above the exit, just big enough to seat one or two people. After that I often climbed up there and gazed down like a gargoyle, eyes fixed on the musicians.

Over those two or three years I saw dozens of bands in the Union Hall. Arkestra. Asia Minor. Baby. Billy TK and The Powerhouse. Blerta. Blue Brick. Butler. Chum. The Country Flyers. Dragon. Farmyard. Highway. Karma. Mammal. 1953 Memorial Society Rock 'n' Roll Band. Olibet. Rockinghorse. Saratoga. Space Farm. Split Ends. Storm. Tamburlaine. Taylor. Ticket. Triangle. Truck. Tapestry. The Windy City Strugglers. There were others whose names I have forgotten or never knew. A few went on to become internationally famous. Dragon and Split Ends – soon to be renamed Split Enz – would find huge success in Australia and beyond. Some of the musicians would become my friends and mentors. Many would vanish into oblivion.

The first band that made a deep impression on me was Tamburlaine. I had got used to the overwhelming volume of most bands, and the way electric guitars and drums seemed to swallow up whatever sound the singer was making, leaving the melody and lyrics sounding like a fly trapped in a glass. (I later learned that this was largely due to the limitations of the PA systems, which were not as sophisticated as they are today.) Tamburlaine didn't suffer from this problem. For a start they had no electric guitars, just several acoustic ones, which they would augment at various times with mandolin or piano. And instead of the typical thundering drummer they had a percussionist, Mark

Hansen, who tapped softly on an assortment of bells, bongos and hand drums.

But the most prominent feature was their singing. Simon Morris, Steve Robinson and Denis Leong, who between them played the various stringed instruments, all had strong voices, which were especially effective when combined in harmony. They did note-perfect versions of 'Your Move' by Yes, and The Moody Blues' 'Legend of a Mind', songs I already knew and liked. But I was even more impressed by the songs I didn't know, which turned out to be ones they had written themselves. Denis Leong had one called 'Pass a Piece of Paper' that might have been Crosby, Stills and Nash on a good day. Simon Morris's 'The Raven and the Nightingale' was as authentically rustic as an old English folk ballad.

There was one band I heard at the Union Hall more often than any other. I intuited that Mammal was the latest evolution of Simon and The Mammals, the band I had seen at the railway station. This was right: Simon Morris had left to form Tamburlaine.

The first time I saw Mammal they were last in a five-band line-up and it was nearly midnight by the time they took the stage. The PA system was groaning with fatigue but they still looked and sounded like a band was supposed to. There were six of them. One guitarist was hunched, bearded and bespectacled, the other rail-thin and barefoot, with eyes lifted to heaven as though in a trance. The pianist pounded inaudibly on an upright, the bass player wore a beret and surveyed the room as though it were an art exhibition, and the drummer hammered his tom-toms with the concentration of a blacksmith at a forge.

Their features were hard to distinguish, partly because of the coloured lights and partly because they were mostly covered with hair. All except for the singer. His name, I learned later, was Rick Bryant. With his short hair and stubbly beard he stood out among this ragtag assortment as he beat a tambourine against his thigh and sang in the kind of aching, rough-textured voice I thought belonged only to old black men from the American South.

Over the next couple of years I would see Mammal at every opportunity. At first I had no idea where the musicians came from, or where they went when they left the Union Hall, but I gradually got to know their names and started to spot them around town. The barefoot guitarist was Robert Taylor. He had a cleaning job in a shoe shop I passed every day on my way to school and I'd see him pushing a floor polisher. The bearded owlish one was Bill Lake. Someone told me he had a philosophy degree. Tony Backhouse was the piano player. While his keyboard was frequently drowned out his voice always cut through, in high clear contrast to Rick's rougher tone.

For a while bass players and drummers came and went from Mammal, but the lasting combination was Mark Hornibrook, whose basslines seemed to have jumped straight from the grooves of a Tamla Motown record, and drummer Kerry Jacobson. Still in his teens, Kerry had only recently left Onslow College and was already the funkiest drummer in Wellington.

As for Rick, seeing him singing in his bodgie uniform of denim jacket and black T-shirt, eyes scrunched tight, I tried to imagine where he might go in the daylight. I could picture him working on the wharves or a construction site, or standing in a

police identity parade. One night my father, having asked the name of the band I was going out to hear, said, 'Oh, Mammal. I work with a bloke who sings in that band. He's a junior lecturer in the English department.'

After that I began to see references to Mammal as a university band. An article about it in the *Listener* in October 1972 was headed 'Dons of Rock'. Most of the musicians had been students at Victoria University when the group started a couple of years earlier. They had formed an alliance with Sam Hunt, a Wellington poet roughly their age, setting some of his lyrics to music and releasing an album that combined their singing with his readings. Their own songs were intricate, with meandering structures, elaborate harmonies and lines that lingered in the memory.

I've been talking to the weather man and he says it's got to change…
There's a whisper of hope in the heart of every man who's hit the ground and stayed down too long…
Hey fella, play nasty for me.

They interspersed originals with a few carefully chosen covers. Once I saw them at the start of a march against the Vietnam War. As the protesters prepared to move off, the band launched into the Stones' 'Street Fighting Man'. It sounded like a call to arms. Most of their covers, though, were by black American artists – The Temptations, Marvin Gaye, Gladys Knight and The Pips. This was unusual for a bunch of Pākehā in the age of acid rock, but the songs made the most of the band's uncommonly supple rhythm section and strong ensemble singing, especially the tender power of Rick's voice.

Listening to Mammal, and Rick in particular, helped shape my idea of what music could be and should be. It could tell a story and make you a part of the story. Rhythm was central: the beat had to move you from the inside out or it meant nothing. But more than anything, what mattered was the quality of the singing. I can only describe Rick's singing as a kind of bruised longing. I began to wonder if this was what people meant when they talked about soul. It became a measure by which I began to judge everything I heard.

After a while, more kids from Onslow started turning up at

the Union Hall. Not everyone came for the music. I'd blunder into couples in dark corners with limbs entwined, or catch the scent of damp burning and see the glowing end of something that was being discreetly passed among a small group. Others would slip outside into the shadows of Mount Street Cemetery to drink Cold Duck or Lion Brown and grope each other among the gravestones.

No one offered me dope but I made myself sick one day smoking tobacco in a pipe I'd taken from my father's study. I was sick again a few weeks later after I drank half a carafe of wine at Peter McLuskie's. But I never got drunk at the Union Hall. That would have seemed like sacrilege: after all, it was my place of worship. And I might have missed some of the music.

Although I was beginning to suffer from occasional bouts of lovesickness, sex only existed somewhere between *The Little Red Schoolbook* and my imagination. One night at the Union Hall a girl from school said, 'Come on, let's dance.' I got to my feet but it felt awkward and wrong. I loved the smell of her long brown hair and the sway of her cotton skirt. I wanted to get closer but I wanted to listen to the band too. How could I do both at the same time?

'I really like the lead guitar part on this song,' I said, shuffling slightly. She looked at me uncomprehendingly, closed her eyes, lifted her arms and carried on dancing – alone.

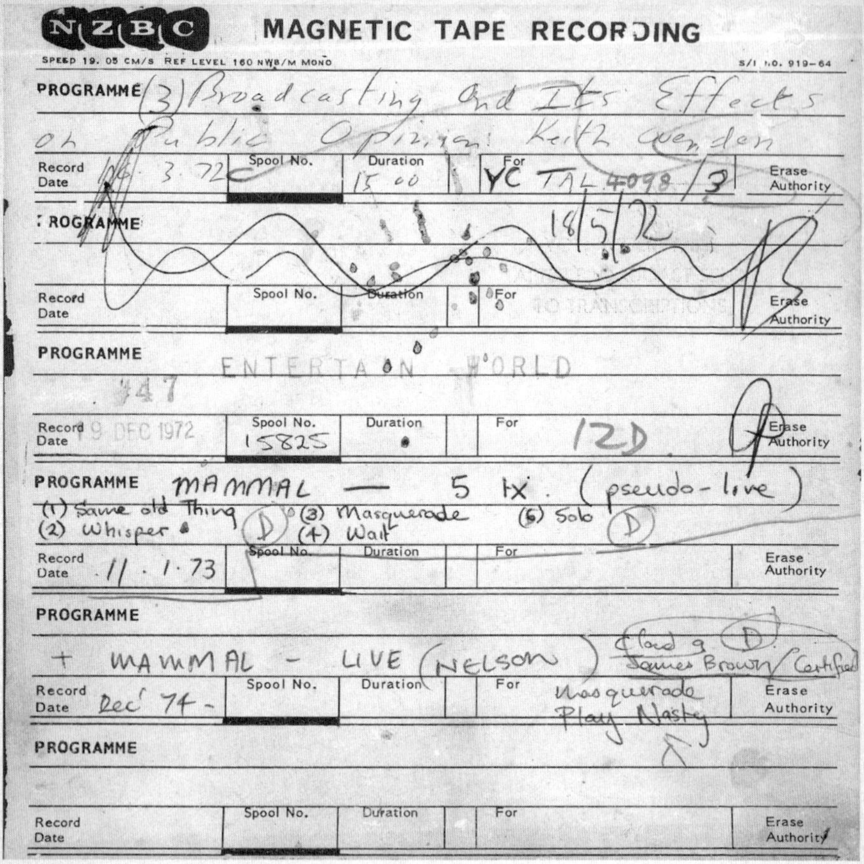

NZBC **MAGNETIC TAPE RECORDING**

SPEED 19. 05 CM/S REF LEVEL 160 NWB/M MONO S/I NO. 919–64

PROGRAMME (3) Broadcasting and Its Effects on Public Opinion: Keith Ovenden

Record Date	Spool No.	Duration		For	Erase Authority
16. 3. 72		15 00		YC TAL 4098 / 3	

18/5/72

PROGRAMME

Record Date	Spool No.	Duration		For	Erase Authority

PROGRAMME ENTERTAIN WORLD

447

Record Date	Spool No.	Duration		For	Erase Authority
19 DEC 1972	15825			12D	

PROGRAMME MAMMAL — 5 tx. (pseudo-live)

(1) Same old Thing (2) Whisper (D) (3) Masquerade (4) Wait (6) Solo (D)

Record Date	Spool No.	Duration		For	Erase Authority
11. 1. 73					

PROGRAMME

+ MAMMAL – LIVE (NELSON) Cloud 9 (D) James Brown / Certified

Record Date	Spool No.	Duration		For	Erase Authority
Dec' 74 –				Masquerade Play Nasty	

PROGRAMME

Record Date	Spool No.	Duration		For	Erase Authority

Hidden track: 'Play Nasty for Me'

Recording is a type of sorcery that allows you to travel through time. It can bring back the breath of the dead, or transport you to a lost moment in adolescence, as I discovered in 2014 when a reel of tape came into my possession. The container – an old box with splitting sides and a peeling label on which 'MAMMAL – LIVE (Nelson) Dec '74' was scrawled in biro – felt magical in my hands. Inside was a shiny brown tape, wound a couple of inches thick around a brittle plastic spool.

This artefact had belonged to Graeme Nesbitt. It was a recording of Mammal, a band of which he was sometimes referred to as manager. It captured them on a typical night away from their Wellington home, playing to an audience of ... well, who exactly? It's hard to tell. There's no applause. Nobody shouts, 'Good evening, Nelson! Are you ready to rock?' so we never know who might have shouted back.

At one point a passing punter finds the microphone that's being used to make the recording – I see it positioned on a solitary stand somewhere in the centre of an old wooden community hall – and, wrapping his entire mouth around its bell, issues a series of primal screams that for maybe twenty seconds almost entirely cancels out the sound of the band. Finally he roars out his only intelligible words, 'MYYYY NAAAAME IIIIS–', at which point someone – I'm guessing Nesbitt – tears the mic away from him, and with it his identity. The band, now in the midst of a stratospheric instrumental, becomes audible again.

I was not in the audience that night in Nelson and yet the sound was strangely and instantly familiar. It was a song I had last heard so long ago I had come to believe I had dreamed it, like the reunion of The Beatles I had watched from the side of the stage until the alarm clock woke me up. Or maybe I had misheard it, and the melody and lyric that had faded in and out of my memory for forty years were quite different from what had actually been sung. The truth is I had never been able to recall many of the words or even much of the tune. Mostly it was just a refrain I had heard at a rock show in the Union Hall one Friday night in my early teens: *Play nasty for me…* And here it was, on the tape.

No wonder the memory was dreamlike. The song itself is a dream. It has its own dream logic in which one place can suddenly become another, and the most improbable group of characters can find themselves in the same story.

It starts out as an old-time country song, a two-step dance tune in attempted four-part harmony. 'Well I'm only the back door to the motel of your heart,' groan the singers, tired and off-key, as though it's three in the morning at the Goneville RSA and there are just two couples shuffling around the dancefloor, clinging to each other to stay upright, and a drunk sprawled out with his head in the bass drum, and the bar manager has told the band that if they want to get paid they've gotta play one more song but if it isn't 'Ten Guitars' then it better be something everyone knows. It is neither, although it could be one of ten thousand country laments.

Well you trampled on my feelings
And you walked across my pride

Now the maître d' has drawn the drapes
On the emptiness inside
And the switchboard that connects your heart to mine
Has broken down somewhere along the line
And the old-time band ignores my heartfelt plea
'Hey fella...
Play nasty for me'

On that last line something unexpected happens. There is a scream, a howl of electricity from centre stage, and the RSA is suddenly a psychedelic ballroom. Robert Taylor, Mammal's lead guitarist, *is* playing nasty. His Stratocaster screams in torment, while somewhere in the background the refrain continues, now a raucous affirmation:

Play nasty for me!

The sleepy country song was just a bluff. The band is wide awake and firing riffs like rockets. And yet this part of the song turns out to be also a bluff. It gives way to a wistful melody sung in half-time:

Homer standing by the plough
He'd go home but he don't know how

Homer? Now what is Homer doing here? This song, in its first three minutes, has already insisted it won't be tethered to the verse–chorus structure of the typical pop song but can and will go anywhere. Now the appearance of the old Greek bard is suggesting not merely a detour but an odyssey. This is borne out over the next twenty-five minutes as this single song journeys through surf music, heavy metal, space jazz, bucolic folk, always trying to get home to that refrain:

Play nasty for me!

In 1974 'Play nasty for me' was more than just a memorable hook in a strange song. It was a pop-cultural joke that the audience that Nelson night would surely have smiled at. *Play Misty for Me*, a film that starred Clint Eastwood and also marked his debut as a director, had recently screened in New Zealand picture theatres. It told the story of a disc jockey stalked by an unhinged fan who obsessively requests the old Errol Garner tune 'Misty'. Working musicians in New Zealand could relate to the disc jockey: they were often subjected as to such demands from drunken audience members. Steve Hemmens, Mammal's first bass player, told me about the night a man wielding a bottle strode up to the bandstand, stood so close they could smell his alcoholic breath, and demanded, 'Play "Help!" or you'll need it.'

Back in the Nelson hall, 'Play Nasty for Me' fills with characters who might be refugees from Bob Dylan's 'Desolation Row'. Homer meets Surfer Joe as Mammal drummer Kerry Jacobson strikes up a pounding tom-tom beat straight off a Surfaris' single, while somewhere a trumpet begins to play 'Oh Mein Papa', as though a bewildered Eddie Calvert has stumbled into the hall and, not realising he is on the wrong stage, whipped out his horn and launched into his 1954 hit.

Calvert was an English trumpet player and all-round entertainer whose successful career had been eclipsed in the 1960s by the rise of pop groups such as The Beatles. But the beat boom wasn't his only bugbear. He was also a vocal opponent of Harold Wilson, Britain's Labour prime minister. By the end of the decade he had decamped to South Africa, where he recorded a version of the hymn 'Amazing Grace', retitled 'Amazing Race' in tribute to Ian Smith's racist Rhodesian government. Around the time of this odious ode, Calvert was hired by Richard Holden, New Zealand Breweries' entertainment manager, to undertake a national tour. He would perform exclusively in taverns booked by Holden.

On the recording it is Mark Hornibrook, Mammal's bass player and former National Youth Orchestra trumpeter, who is blowing the horn, but the fact Calvert was touring the country just when Mammal were traipsing through the backblocks is one of those coincidences on which the surreal world of 'Play Nasty for Me' is built.

We then hear a singer, probably Tony Backhouse, joining the chorus of 'Oh Mein Papa' in a full fruity tenor, like a drunken Eddie Fisher, whose vocal version of the same song had been a hit just a year before Calvert's. Eventually the two Eddies realise they are in the wrong song, the wrong city, the wrong universe, and head for the exit as Robert Taylor launches into a twanging riff reminiscent of Dick Dale, King of the Surf Guitar, which he concludes with a long scrape down the E-string, aimed at driving these interlopers out the door. Things gradually settle into a circular sequence of chords as Taylor solos, now using his wah-wah pedal to lend his notes a snarling tone that says, 'Fuck off, and don't come back!'

Musical worlds continue to collide and collapse into each other. Guitar menace dissolves into smooth Buffalo Springfield-style harmony, which is in turn overpowered by rock-a-boogie as someone begins to wail the white man's blues, until the whole thing unwinds again into cacophony. Strings bend and squeal and a saxophone shrieks like a cat in heat. 'It must be all them drugs they are taking,' mutters what might be a bewildered onlooker but is in fact Rick Bryant. Hornibrook, now back on bass, lets his fingers wander abstractedly about the fretboard. Guitars chime and familiar chords start to emerge from the murk. It's that old chorus again, although no one is singing it now. One of the guitars insinuates the 'Play nasty' riff and we're back into the theme for a few bars. There's another scream, a few more stanzas of four-part harmony, guitars again, with Taylor accelerating his solo until it soars. Someone starts playing the riff of The Beatles' 'Day Tripper', which only spurs Taylor on. And then, with a final purgative howl, Bryant vomits out the chorus one last time.

Iwantyoutoplaynastyformenastyformenastyforme
yayayyayyarrrghhhh…

In a heroic climax, Kerry Jacobson pummels his drums in a series of John Bonham-style ba-da-la-bump-ba-da-la-bumps and the song comes to an end, followed by … nothing. Twenty years of popular music – if not the entire history of lyric poetry, from Homer to Lennon – have flashed past in twenty-five minutes and no one seems to have noticed. The silence that follows could almost be the story of New Zealand rock in the early '70s. While the Breweries circuit hosted covers acts, showbands and faded offshore entertainers such as Eddie Calvert, original groups were forced to create their own circuit: provincial halls, university campuses, unlicensed clubs, occasional festivals, street parties. Little of their music ever found its way on to disc.

'Play Nasty for Me' is sui generis, a singular, extraordinary piece of work. No record was ever released, no studio recording ever made. There is nowhere on the planet, other than a half-empty hall in Nelson that night in 1974, where you would have heard this. It was the age of the rock epic. British prog-rock groups such as Pink Floyd and Yes were creating suites that took up entire sides of albums, but 'Play Nasty for Me' had little in common with these. What it did resemble – slightly – was the early work of Frank Zappa and The Mothers of Invention, full of collage and jump-cuts, or The Beatles, whose 'Happiness Is a Warm Gun' packed a genre tour of folk, hard rock and doo-wop into three minutes. It was a dialectic of pop, pitched from a place at the bottom of the world, upside down in the middle of nowhere, so far off the map that normal rules didn't apply. It could have happened only somewhere the stakes were so low that a band, suddenly realising it could do anything it liked because nobody was watching and nobody cared, grasped that freedom with the full strength of its imagination and created a work of art that would be almost forgotten for forty years.

The tape seems to have ended. All is silent except for the gentle swishing of the spool. Then, as if from the far end of a cave, can be heard shouts, shuffling, a few desultory claps. Who were these people? Did they know what they had witnessed? Rick Bryant mutters just off mic, 'Goodnight. See you later. Thanks for sticking round,' and the tape runs off its spool.

06
'YOU CAN'T DRESS LIKE THAT IN THE HUTT'

When I first saw Graeme Nesbitt on the Union Hall stage it took me a few moments to realise he was the same man I'd seen a couple of years earlier cutting the ribbon at the Railway Station. Standing in the spotlight, he appeared to be glowing. He was dressed all in white, but it wasn't just the clothes or the light, or the way his long hair and dark beard gave him a Jesus look. Back then a lot of people looked like Jesus. Although I didn't know it, the glowing man introducing the bands that night was the reason there *were* bands in the Union Hall.

I had sensed that what I had been seeing were local variants of the happenings taking place in San Francisco, London or New York, which I had read about. But I was yet to appreciate that each happening had a quality of its own, partly shaped by the imaginations of the individuals involved, people like Graeme Nesbitt. Not only did Nesbitt organise almost all the rock concerts at the Union Hall between 1970 and 1974, he pioneered a performance circuit that provided a launch pad for a handful of New Zealand groups who dared to make their own music – at a time when to play anything other than cover versions of current hits normally rendered a band or solo musician unemployable.

To find out more about the man who had been responsible for much of the soundtrack to my teenage years, I am driving towards Upper Hutt. Graeme Nesbitt lived here as a teenager. His father Robert, now in his nineties, still lives here, as does Rob, the eldest of Graeme's three younger brothers. I have arranged to meet Rob at Classic Cycles, the workshop where he prepares and repairs vintage motorcycles for racing. 'I'll take you to meet Dad,' he had barked down the phone. 'Since Mum died you can talk to him about anything you like. I tell him Graeme kept the New Zealand music industry going by selling pot and he just laughs.'

From State Highway Two on a misty Sunday morning, the Hutt Valley looks still and peaceful, a scattering of silent suburbs across a pretty floodplain. And yet when I think of the Hutt I remember violence. My Onslow days were haunted by legends of Hutt Valley gangs storming into Wellington on weekends, looking for schoolboys to beat up.

And then there had been my first professional gig. By the time I'd been at Onslow for a couple of years my attempts to learn the bass had led to my joining a series of school bands with ever-changing names and line-ups. The most ambitious of these had answered a newspaper ad that invited groups to audition for a 'Teenage Dance'. Surprisingly, we got the gig and found ourselves one Saturday night in a vast concrete gymnasium in the Hutt Valley suburb of Taita. There were two other bands.

One was a local outfit that played lacklustre covers of current hits (their best song was 'Helen Wheels' by Paul McCartney and Wings). Their singer had brought along a three-foot polystyrene phallus, which he occasionally picked up and waved around on stage. The other band was fronted by three Māori cousins from Ruatoki, an isolated village in Urewera Valley, where English was still a second language, if spoken at all. They played a version of 'All Along the Watchtower' that scorched like a blowtorch.

As the lights dimmed and Hutt Valley teenagers began to fill the hall, it became apparent the crowd was dividing along territorial lines, one tribe gathering along the left-hand wall, the other along the right. I never found out whether the division represented different schools or warring neighbourhoods but violence seemed inevitable. We were on first. We sat backstage with the other bands and discussed strategies for survival.

'When they start fighting, you keep playing. And if they get onstage, whatever you do, don't stop,' one of the Māori guitarists said.

'So that's what you'd do?' I asked nervously.

'No,' he said. He grinned. 'I'd hit 'em. Don't you try that though. Just keep playing. We'll keep 'em off the stage.'

Sure enough, our first note was the cue for the fighting to begin. The stage lights made it hard to see what was going on, but looking up from the fretboard, where I was shakily fingering the bassline to 'Rock 'n' Roll Hoochie Coo', I was aware of movement that didn't seem like dancing. There were shouts and the quick flash of glass.

We didn't play well, although fear enlivened our normally sluggish tempos. In the end only Boyd, our stylish saxophone player who was dressed for the occasion in pink velvet trousers, incurred injury. Crossing the hall after our performance, he was butted in the head by a Huttite who was heard to mutter, almost apologetically, 'You can't dress like that in the Hutt, mate.'

In Upper Hutt I pull into a petrol station and ask the attendant for directions to Ward Street. 'You a writer?' he asks, and I wonder what it is that has telegraphed so clearly my identity and purpose. Is it something I'm wearing? It turns out he knows the Nesbitts. Rob had mentioned someone was coming up from Wellington to talk to him.

I find Rob in his workshop. There are disassembled bikes in corners, engines on benches, wheels suspended from rafters, miscellaneous parts stacked floor to ceiling on shelves. Everything is silver, dulled with oil. Rob is big, bearded and ponytailed, arms blue with tattoos, a textbook biker. His voice rumbles like a Norton engine. I recognise him as one of the bouncers I've been seeing at concerts since the days of the Union Hall. He tells me he usually works security with his two younger brothers, Bruce and Greg. Once, after a ZZ Top show in Auckland, the three of them were invited to a party in a downtown nightclub. Somehow they managed to commandeer a limousine. When they disembarked outside the club, a girl rushed up and kissed Greg, thanking him for a great concert. Inside, another woman embraced Rob. 'So where are you guys from?' she asked. 'Ah, Upper Hutt.' She was confused. 'But you're from Texas though, right?' 'Nah, we're from Taita.'

Their brother Graeme would never have been mistaken for a member of ZZ Top. When Rob takes me to his father's home

I notice on the wall a life-sized portrait in pastels of the four brothers, and am told it was painted in Borneo in the 1980s when they went there together to hunt tigers. In the picture Rob, Bruce and Greg look like the bikers they are. Graeme, cool and clean-shaven, might be a 1940s film star.

He was always different, Rob and his father agree. His gifts for language and literature had been recognised in primary school, when the family was living in rural Kohukohu in the Hokianga, where Robert Snr was postmaster. Advised by his teachers that the local school, Rawene District High, would not be able to extend him to his full potential, Graeme's parents sent him to board in Whangarei – the nearest major town and a full day's journey away on gravel roads – so he could attend Boys High.

While his brothers dreamed teenage dreams of motorcycles and mayhem, Graeme studied Latin, grew his hair long and got hooked on pop music. His interest in music had already kicked in at Kohukohu with *The Lever Hit Parade* and *The Sunset Show* on Radio 1ZB, and he had taken guitar lessons from George Sutherland, a teacher at Rawene High who was involved in national kapa haka competitions. In Whangarei he befriended Reggie Ruka, the leading local guitarist and singer. Graeme started following Reggie from gig to gig, picking up the basis of his repertoire. Sometimes he would head into Auckland to hear other live performers or for a big show like The Beatles' 1964 descent on the Auckland Town Hall.

In 1965 Robert Snr took a job as an instructor in postal services and the family moved to Upper Hutt, where they were put up at Trentham Military Camp. Graeme's room was an old laundry, about thirty feet long, where he could play music day or night without disturbing anyone. He filled it with musical instruments and equipment. His brothers recall him owning, and to some degree mastering, six- and twelve-string guitars, violin, saxophone and bass, but his preference, formed in part by the Māori singers he grew up amongst, was for folk and country songs, which he played on the guitar. At Upper Hutt College his friends included Ray Mercer, a guitarist who would later be a member of national hitmakers The Dedikation, and bass player Alastair Richardson, who would leave school to join and co-write most of the hits for The Fourmyula, New Zealand's most successful recording band of the late 1960s.

With another classmate, Christine Klocek, he formed a duo, Los Pescadores, named for a song on an album by the Native American folk singer Buffy Sainte-Marie. By the time they were out of school the pair, dressed in home-made ponchos, were performing regularly at Wellington coffee houses such as Monde Marie and Chez Paree. They even appeared on a children's television programme. At school Graeme had faced suspension for refusing a haircut; now he looked like a cross between a flower child and a South American revolutionary, sporting beard, beret and a preference for purple. Starting at Victoria University in 1968 he became involved in the University Folk Club as both promoter and performer. When international folk stars such as Julie Felix and Peter, Paul and Mary toured he would help out any way he could.

It was around this time that Graeme's path intersected with that of a fellow student and aspiring musician who would go on to become his flatmate, bandmate, cellmate and lifelong friend.

07
EVANGELISTS

Rick Bryant grew up on Wellington's south coast and went to Rongotai College, where he developed the persona of a surly rebel. This masked an inherent shyness. The first time Rick agreed to sing in public he spent the previous day in a state of terror. Once he got up on stage his fears did not depart, but he realised singing was the thing he had been put on Earth to do.

Rick's musical tastes were already skewed towards black American music – blues, soul, gospel – and the more credible of its white interpreters. He had first sung in the mid 1960s with The Changing Ways, a band composed mainly of Onslow College students, but had left after a difference of opinion with their leader, Simon Morris, over the music of The Pretty Things. Rick admired the English rock band's raw bluesy edge; Simon didn't think their songs had any place in Changing Ways' repertoire. Rick had gone on to sing with Gutbucket, a New Plymouth blues band that had recently relocated to Wellington, and Original Sin, a group that included Morris, along with a recent arrival from Australia, Bill Lake.

When Rick first saw Graeme sometime in 1968, the poncho did not make a good impression. Nor did the music. To Rick, the folk sounds favoured by Graeme were fey and effete, and he couldn't resist mocking Los Pescadores for their outfits and faux Mexican name, which he would mispronounce variously as Los Disasteros, Los Pistachios and Los Pecorinos. But there was a lot Rick and Graeme had in common. For one thing, they were both ferociously academic. For another, they were both interested in drugs. During his first year as a student Rick had been offered a joint and found he liked it – a lot. Before long he was ensuring himself a cheap regular supply and supplementing his university bursary by selling it.

Graeme was doing the same. More outgoing than Rick, he also became something of a proselytiser for marijuana. In late 1969 he was appointed to a committee of the Victoria University Students Association to look into the question of legalisation. Under the existing law, the cultivation, possession, use and sale of the drug were illegal. The committee formed the opinion this had to change. It recommended controlled use of marijuana should be legalised.

The only member of the committee without a legal background, Graeme nevertheless became its spokesperson. 'The older generation has a fear of being exposed by the younger generation,' the *Evening Post* reported him saying in April 1970. 'They escape truths about themselves ... While eager to retain their social stimulus, alcohol, they are vehemently opposed to the recognition of marijuana as the social stimulus of the young.'

He advocated 'controlled use'. Marijuana should be available to those over the legal drinking age. People should be able to be convicted of being 'stoned and disorderly'. To keep the drug out of the hands of peddlers and inhibit smuggling, it should be illegal to buy or sell it.

Convinced that fairness and social justice could be achieved more quickly if everyone smoked pot, Rick and Graeme saw themselves as evangelists. Before long they were flatting together in a three-storey house above Aro Valley. Through Wellington's small enclave of cannabis users, Rick was soon offered other substances to buy and sell. Wary of LSD and fearful of hypodermic needles, he refused. Graeme, on the other hand, seemed willing to try anything. Rick was at home one night studying Chaucer when the phone rang. 'Your mate has OD'd,' the caller said. 'You'd better come and get him.'

Rick hurried to a house in central Wellington, where he found Graeme conscious, but only just. The junkies with him advised Rick the way to keep him alive was to support his weight and keep him walking. Eventually he got Graeme home and went to bed, only to be woken at regular intervals throughout the night by the sound of his flatmate painfully retching out a window. Rick believes Graeme never used intravenous drugs again, although he remembers him taking LSD before attempting maths assignments. When Graeme slept – which he didn't seem to do often – he would wear headphones, through which he would soothe his subconscious with reel-to-reel recordings copied from long-playing records of the Royal Shakespeare Company.

While Rick pursued his love of blues, Graeme continued to play folk and country music. He joined forces with folk singer Max Winnie, jazz bassist Colin Heath and harmonica player Andrew Delahunty as Country Deal; in 1971 the group appeared on the television talent quest Studio One, becoming finalists, and made an album, *Max, Colin & Graeme with Andrew*, for Kiwi Records. The album featured liner notes by Rick Bryant, and Graeme would become part of Rick's next musical project, Rick and The Rockets. The psychedelic rock group's brief but remarkable career included a summer residency at a bohemian café, Chez Eelco in Nelson, and a performance at the 1969 National Blues Convention in Auckland – of which more later.

Drugs and rock music were still very much minority pursuits but the counterculture was growing, particularly around university campuses. By the late 1960s, student newspapers had begun to take on the characteristics of the underground papers overseas. An issue of *Salient* ran a two-page article about the pros and cons of drug use. With text printed in purple against a chaotic red collage, the spread did a good job of simulating the effects of a hallucinogenic experience but was entirely illegible.

On other pages, between reprints of Gilbert Shelton's *Fabulous Furry Freak Brothers* comics, you could find in-depth discussions of the Vietnam War, the anti-nuclear movement, apartheid, contraception and sexual politics. Many of the radical figures afforded space in the pages of these student papers, and so effectively leading student opinion, were a generation older than the students. They included doctor and social critic Erich Geiringer and poet turned prophet James K. Baxter.

Flicking through editions from the time, you might think local rock music was having little impact on university life: alongside an occasional report of a classical concert or experimental performance, the music most frequently mentioned was folk. Untainted by commerce, associated with left-wing politics, and carrying a touch of hipness thanks to Bob Dylan, folk appealed to the idealistic and the high-minded. Folk clubs sprang up. Simon Morris, Bill Lake and Robert Taylor all made their campus debuts at folk concerts.

The bridge between the worlds of folk and rock was blues. Although blues experienced mild resistance from a few English traditionalists – the ones Rick Bryant called 'the pound of fatty bacon and a pint of good ale brigade' – folkies, by and large, recognised it as the authentic expression of an oppressed and disenfranchised people and therefore a form of folk, even if its local variant was being performed by middle-class bohemians whose experience of cotton fields and killing floors was inevitably limited.

Involved first with the University Folk Club, Graeme Nesbitt went on to establish the Victoria University Rock and Blues Society – having the word 'blues' in there gave the organisation a necessary veneer of respectability – and began to put on concerts in the Union Hall. These were unlike anything you'd experience if you went to see a band in a pub or in most of the city's nightclubs. Although the music could be bluesy, it was seldom strictly blues. Like the underground and progressive rock shows of Britain and the US, there was a heavy emphasis on musicianship, the songs were long, and the bands were defiantly non-commercial.

Similar scenes were developing in other cities. Dunedin, too, had an underground rock institution, Otago University's Blues Rock Club, which hosted local bands such as Lutha and Pussyfoot. In Christchurch, guitarist Eddie Hansen and Auckland drummer Rick Ball, both of whom had been in radio-friendly pop groups – The Revival and The Challenge, respectively – were developing their brand of psychedelic rock in Ticket, with a residency at a nightclub called Aubrey's, a favourite haunt of American servicemen on R&R leave from Vietnam.

In Auckland, blues-rock had snuck on to campus through another quasi-respectable institution: poetry. The campus poets were more militant and had an even more clearly defined agenda than the musicians. 'Poetry was a practice run for a complete change of consciousness,' poet Alan Brunton would recall in his 1997 memoir *Years Ago Today*. Brunton had left his hometown of Hamilton in the late 1960s looking for 'a life of imagination'. He didn't find it in Auckland University's history department, where lecturer Michael Bassett summarised New Zealand history as 'roads and bridges', nor in the English department, where a senior tutor advised him to drop out while he could still get his fees refunded.

During a 1969 hitchhiking trip between Wellington and Auckland, Brunton and his friend Jim Stevenson formed what Brunton called the 'paradigmatic model for the restitution of New Zealand in an alternative universe'. They declared: 'The shift would begin with the Imagination and be at the hands of the Cultural Liberation Front. The CLF would infiltrate administrations through their weakest link, their cultural clubs and societies.'

Meetings of the CLF were held at Brunton's home, 5 Boyle Crescent, Grafton, one of two neighbouring crash pads managed by James K. Baxter. Its first event was a concert in Auckland University's Student Union Hall. It featured the Original Sun Blues Band, with poetry readings by Brunton, David Mitchell and Russell Haley, and a performance piece that involved all three poets, one reading aloud while another stood in a tin bathtub being soaped by the third. Several more such events followed until the university banned them.

In 1970 Graeme Nesbitt was elected Victoria University's cultural affairs officer and appointed controller of the National Student Arts Festival, which it was Victoria's turn to host. Until four years earlier the weekend festival had been run as an adjunct to the New Zealand Universities Winter Tournament, at which sports teams from the various universities competed and socialised and breweries did well. Nineteen sixty-six had seen the birth of the New Zealand Universities Arts Council as a standing committee of the University Students Association, with a brief to promote student cultural affairs at a national level. The arts festival was to be its prime focus.

Early festivals featured film, drama, poetry, chess, and classical, jazz and folk music. Anything resembling rock was confined to a 'hop' on the Saturday night. This began to change with the 1968 festival, which was held in Auckland. 'Unlike previous Arts Festivals and Tournaments,' the student newspaper *Craccum* reported, 'Auckland's … effort is to have no traditional hop. Instead there will be a Freak Out.'

Plans for this had been outlined to *Craccum* by the festival's social controller, Malcolm Calder. It would be modelled on similar functions in America. Acid-rock and way-out blues would provide the base, supplemented by psychedelic lighting and a turned-on atmosphere. Instead of the usual 'bleary, boozy, small-town-type dance', the social programme would be

I NEED YOU!
200 of you. I need students to answer phones, sell advertising, build bridges, dance naked, arrange deals and have a great time. Arts Festival and I need you. See me at the Gymnasium (till noon each day) or ring 70.319 or leave your name and phone number at the Students' Association office.
Grame Nesbitt
Arts Festival Controller

enhanced by something with 'depth and meaning in itself as well as entertainment value'.

Whether the freak out lived up to Calder's promise was a matter of contention. The *Craccum* reviewer Bill Mandle seemed simultaneously prudish and blasé. After complaining there had been 'too many boobs', he griped that the event 'had all the respectability of a *Herald* editorial, without even the latter's lurking sense of menace'. Mandle didn't bother to name any of the bands or musicians who had played, merely describing the music as 'a mannered wailing, lacking either the virtues or vices of pop or jazz'. The guy obviously knew how to enjoy himself. Summing up the festival as a whole, he asked rhetorically: 'Anything sinister ... ? Probably too much pot – the transfusion from Victoria proving too much at times for the recently starved Aucklanders.'

It is not recorded what Mandle thought of the 1969 festival, which was hosted by Otago University. A couple of busloads of students from Auckland made the long journey south, while a contingent from Wellington included Graeme Nesbitt and Rick Bryant. Rick was booked to play with The Windy City Strugglers. Graeme was attending as an observer: he had been appointed controller for the following year's festival.

Graeme's vision for 1970 was to create the biggest freak out yet. It would be inspired by happenings overseas – Woodstock had taken place in upstate New York the August before – plus some homegrown pranksterism of his own. A special shipment of cannabis from overseas was arranged, and two students collected it from a visiting ship. A full-page ad in *Salient* showed Graeme Nesbitt in full Che Guevara get-up, eyeballing and pointing at the viewer like Uncle Sam. The text read: 'I NEED YOU! 200 of you. I need students to answer phones, sell advertising, build bridges, dance naked, arrange deals and have a great time. Arts Festival and I need you.'

08
PETER F. AND THE LIGHTS

As a serious young student of rock I would pore over any information I could find that might deepen my impression of a band or piece of music. Often that wasn't much. On the back cover of Highway's sole and self-titled album, in white type on bright purple, was a dedication to a list of people who had assisted the band in various ways. In 1971 I knew it by heart. The contributions noted were vague – 'Steve the roadie' ... 'Gary the hassler' ... 'Alan who tried' – as though to give any more detail would be to expose some secret. Or perhaps it was just that no one could remember. Some names conjured up glamorous images of people I imagined must be part of Highway's retinue: 'Hans and Aveleen'... 'Roger and Anastasia'... 'Siddhartha'. And then there was 'Peter F. and the lights'. Peter Frater's lights were legendary. Seeing his credit on the *Highway* cover, I realised the mind-bending projections I'd seen at the Union Hall must have been his handiwork.

Four and a half decades later Frater, now well into seventies, is still working in concert production as stage-door keeper at Wellington's Opera House and St James Theatre. When I meet him at a café in Island Bay he tells me that the music business never provided the means for a comfortable retirement, and its family-unfriendly hours have left him unattached and undomesticated. His eyebrows are anarchic and he wears his long hair tied back, as he has done since the days of Highway. He calls himself a Wellington cockney: he was born in the city and has stayed here all his life.

'I always wanted to have an involvement with performance,' he says. 'I started off in high school Gilbert and Sullivan, the annual productions, and then I tried youth theatre, which was a very arty thing to be doing at the time. Basically I tried singing, dancing and acting and didn't scratch the surface on those three, but I did have a talent for putting on events and an interest in technology.'

Frater got involved with the Contemporary Arts Group, a cultural club at Victoria University that put on variety shows. At that point in the mid '60s, folk music was as hip as it got. Through the university folk scene he met Max Winnie and Graeme Nesbitt. In 1970 Nesbitt called on his services. He was determined to create the biggest scene yet and needed Peter's help. Arts festivals had always included some music – along with poetry readings, drama productions, chess tournaments and oratory contests – but this year the music was to be the centrepiece. And the focus had shifted from folk and the occasional classical or jazz concert to the newly named rock.

The high point – in every sense – would be a rock concert at Paramount Theatre, headlined by a new band Nesbitt had come across. Highway consisted of five Wellington musicians, all still in their teens or early twenties yet already with years of professional experience among them. Guitarist Phil Pritchard and bass player George Limbidis had just returned from stints with Sydney bands. Drummer Jim Lawrie had played with Pritchard at youth club dances around Wellington while still at school. Second guitarist George Barris had been in Auckland playing bass with Bruno Lawrence and Chris Seresin in Fresh Air, and Bruce Sontgen had sung with the then disbanded Tom Thumb.

At first Highway played just for themselves, night after night behind the closed doors of a Lambton Quay rehearsal room. Money or even an audience were hardly in their thoughts. Rather than start by learning covers, like every previous band they had been in, Highway made original music from the outset. Organic compositions that started from a bluesy riff of Pritchard's or a bassline of Limbidis's grew into multi-part opuses that kept expanding as long as the musicians felt inspired. A single song might stretch to three-quarters of an hour, although no one was keeping track of the time.

The festival was a success. Consciousnesses were altered, minds blown. It even turned a respectable profit. As Nesbitt had predicted, Highway's Paramount debut had been the centrepiece. It had sold out, leaving queues outside unable to get in. A second show had been hastily arranged. Many people simply left the theatre, paid for the second show and filed back inside. The band was phenomenally tight, even compared to overseas blues-rock groups. More than that, there was something about Highway that perfectly matched the mood of the student crowd. It had broken free of music's false restraints. If everyone followed the music, perhaps society's restraints could be cast off as well.

Peter Frater remembers it as an epiphany. That night at the Paramount he had set up and operated the lights. He hadn't done anything fancy, merely splashed some colours around the stage. But Highway's performance and the crowd's reaction had got him thinking. From photographs and film clips he had formed an idea of the type of light shows bands were using overseas, and how such effects might be achieved. A couple of nights later he visited Highway at their rehearsal room and let them know what he had in mind.

Soon afterwards, when Highway set out on a tour of university campuses, Frater accompanied them. He brought an assortment of lights, as well as movie, slide and overhead projectors. Someone else brought the pot. 'We were evangelists,' he says with a twinkle, and raises his hands like a preacher.

When the band returned to Wellington, leaving in its wake a trail of stoned disciples, Frater brought his ever-expanding light show to Lucifer's, the latest in a series of clubs catering to Wellington's burgeoning counterculture. Lucifer's had been set up in the loft of an old stable in central Wellington by Dave Day, a Highway fan and sometime carpet layer. Over the next nine months Highway played there frequently. Newspaper ads for Lucifer's used coded language to let the freaks and hippies know this was their scene. 'Especially for the cool people' and 'Lucifer's for friendly peaceful people,' the straplines ran. The venue was unlicensed but alcohol was hardly missed. Musician Chris Prowse, who went there often, told me, 'Alcohol was considered uncool. We looked down on people who drank. We called them pissheads.'

Sometimes Nesbitt would arrange what he promoted with droll humour as a 'joint venture' between Lucifer's and the University Blues Society: bands would play half the evening at the Union Hall and then move to Lucifer's and continue until around dawn. One memorable evening someone dressed in a Tinkerbell costume and sporting a prominent five o'clock shadow unexpectedly descended via a hoist from the ceiling, throwing out fistfuls of hand-rolled joints.

Meanwhile Frater continued to perfect his light show. 'I used to make my own oil wheels,' he says. 'I didn't come up with how to make the cassettes – someone else figured that out. You have to have two concentric cells, and he came up with the bright idea of using ball bearings so you could spin the things around. The electric motors were out of meters or timing devices.

'Then there was another type using a couple of bits of slide glass, sprinkling on some effervescent salts and a couple of drops of coloured oil, whacking them together. Add the heat of the lamp – they were the great explosions. It was messy and there had to be at least one person on each projector. In the end I probably had about a dozen up and running. I could do a whole hall. I used to use 16-mm film as well. Another thing was to get an overhead projector and get a handful of crawling live insects – wetas, slaters – and throw them on the platter.

'It was pretty labour-intensive,' he continues, 'probably about half a dozen people. And there were always things like the motors would stop or the lamp would blow. Getting shocks. Something would be working, suddenly it would stop, someone would touch it, there'd be a flash and a puff of smoke and someone yelling "Fuck!"'

I wondered about the ultraviolet lights and bright tunnels of sheets. 'That was just old theatrical hokum,' he says. 'Ultraviolet had been around for years. You got a white sheet and washed it in Lux soap flakes, you got the cloth loaded up with the soap, and the soap had a brightening agent in it. That's the trick – brightening agents act amazingly under ultraviolet light. If you looked into the light your head started to go …' He mimes a brain exploding, and grins.

Highway didn't stick around Wellington for long. By the time I started going to the Union Hall they were in Australia, where they soon fell apart. But I did see them play once. It was at a hippie wedding on a spring afternoon in the garden of a crumbling Wellington villa. I had tagged along with friends who attended an alternative school where the barefooted bride was a teacher. The band played outdoors and I was spellbound. It was a crucial step towards a world of music that, over the next two or three years, I would study intently at close range.

09
INCREASING SOPHISTICATION

There was another place where bands played. It was the pub, and you had to be twenty to get in. Even if I'd been old enough I might still have been turned away on account of the way I looked, as would most of the crowd I mingled with at the Union Hall. Signs at the entrances to the lounge bars where the bands played read 'Neat Dress Essential' and surly bouncers enforced the policy. Whatever music was being made in those pubs, it seemed to be for a different New Zealand.

Until the late 1960s the pubs rarely had music at all: they closed by six in the evening, well before the hour at which drink and song normally exercise their mutual attraction. It had been that way since 1917 when, under pressure from the powerful temperance movement, wartime regulations were introduced to curtail hotel licensing hours. It was presumably felt it would be unseemly for people in the home country to drink up large while their countrymen were dying by the thousands in trenches in France and Belgium.

After the war the regulations were left in place for fifty years, but if they were supposed to curb the excesses of Kiwi drinkers they had the opposite effect. In a phenomenon that became known as the six o'clock swill, men (and they were all men) would hit the bars at the end of the working day and try to consume as much liquor as possible before the publican turfed them out at six. I have a memory of sitting in our Ford Prefect in Molesworth Street as a preschooler, waiting for my mother who had gone into a dairy to get something for dinner, and seeing a tide of men dressed in grey surging from the front doors of a building with darkened windows. The way the men spilling across the footpath and into the street were stumbling and shouting made me want to slide down the seat and hide on the floor.

'What are those men doing?' I asked my mother when she returned. 'It's all right, darling,' she said, 'they've just come out of the pub.'

A year or two later I got a glimpse of what went on behind those doors. I'd been out for the afternoon with Dad, and now a friend of Dad's and the friend's young daughter were giving us a lift home. The car stopped. 'Wait here, we'll only be a few minutes,' Dad's friend said. The two men disappeared inside a dark-windowed building. The minutes grew longer. The girl, who was a little older than me, got sick of playing 'I Spy' and decided to scare me. 'You know,' she said, in a whisper that carried a terrifying authority, 'some men never come out of those places.'

In a flash I was out of the car and in through the door of the hotel, pushing my way through the crowd of men, looking for my father. I found him standing near the bar. He carried me back to the car and assured me he would definitely be coming out of

the place very soon, and we would be going home – where, if I was good, maybe I could listen to some of my Beatles records before bed.

Public bars were utilitarian places. All the licence-holder needed was a brew, a bowser and a barman. The range of beverages on offer was extremely limited. The main one was beer, poured from hoses into big glass jugs. As most of the pubs were controlled by one or other of the country's two major beer companies, Dominion Breweries and New Zealand Breweries, there was no incentive to offer variety. Over the years these monopolists had bought up most of the smaller regional breweries around the country and absorbed them into their empires. (In 1977 New Zealand Breweries changed its name to Lion Breweries.)

There were no tables or chairs. You could pack more drinkers

bottle sales
drive in

FINE GRAIN

in standing than seated so why waste space? Floors were concrete or tiled, much like you would find in a public toilet; all you needed was a hose to wash away the spilt beer, blood, piss and spew at closing time. Women were seldom seen. An Act had been passed in 1910 making it illegal to employ women in bars, apart from members of the licensee's family and barmaids already employed the year before. Pubs rarely sold food. Who was going to waste precious drinking time eating? Anyway, The Wife would be waiting at home with meat and three veg on the table, ready for The Husband when he staggered through the door.

It was ironic that this culture of desperate excess had resulted from the efforts of prohibitionists and temperance lobbyists, and doubly ironic that the restrictions benefited the makers and marketers of alcohol. As the bars were strictly functional, in much the same way as pigsties and milking sheds are, there was no need to make them attractive so the owners saved on furnishings, décor and maintenance. And with such a huge chunk of the sales concentrated into a single hour of the day – between five and six o'clock – staffing costs were kept to a minimum. When a change to the Act in 1961 made the employment of barmaids legal again, it offered yet another cost-saving option: hotel owners paid them less than barmen.

Still, the return of the barmaids was a harbinger of change. With the growth of air travel, the disparity between New Zealand's drinking laws and those of Europe and the United States was becoming more obvious. There were growing calls to revise the liquor laws. At the 1967 general election a referendum was held. It came out three-to-one in favour of reform.

Licensing hours were extended to ten p.m. and the breweries

were forced to rethink the nature of their establishments. To remain viable, pubs now needed to be places that attracted both men and women, offered a comprehensive night out, and provided food and entertainment. In Molesworth Street, on the site of the old Metropolitan Hotel where, as a child, I had first witnessed the swill, rose the brand new Lion Tavern, a two-storey concrete edifice with a private bar named Spectrum decked out for dancing. For a cover charge of 75 cents, from Monday to Saturday you could enjoy live music interspersed with records played by DJs from seven to ten at night. On Saturdays there were free matinees. Peter Frater installed a light show, although nothing as mind-bending as his campus illuminations.

'Kiwi' Keith Holyoake, the prime minister, attended the opening with his daughter Keitha, and praised the new building as an 'addition to the gaiety and increasing sophistication of our city'. The gaiety and sophistication went only so far. Each night at closing time the bar manager would switch on an ear-splitting siren to encourage patrons to swiftly vacate the premises.

The Spectrum Bar was a model that would be replicated many times. In a real-life game of Monopoly, Dominion and Lion both began buying up and adapting hotels around the country. Sometimes an old hotel would be demolished and a new one built. Lion established its own architectural department.

As most communities opposed public drinking in residential areas, the new taverns were usually sited some distance from town, often on a busy stretch of highway. Large car parks enabled drinkers to drive there and back. It was too far to walk. Anyway by night's end many of them were barely able to stand.

10
GLAM ROCK AND FANTASMAGORICAL HUGGLEMAFLOPS

Like most New Zealanders, my first encounter with Alastair Riddell was in my own living room, in black and white. The tall androgynous figure with dark tresses, silver eyeshadow and white satin bell-bottoms, with a scarf trailing almost to the floor, pouted and preened his way through a song that seemed to be an ode to a drag queen. It was 1974 and Riddell was making his debut with his band Space Waltz on the nationally televised *New Faces* talent quest.

His appearance caused visible discomfort among the all-male judging panel. 'This effeminate thing is very commercial in the heavy area,' 2ZB DJ Paddy O'Donnell blathered incoherently. Entertainer Howard Morrison batted his eyelids and blew mock kisses. But Riddell had caught a glam rock wave the country seemed ready for. 'Out on the Street' was released as a single just days later, and became the first local No. 1 hit in four years.

At sixteen I watched *New Faces* not with high expectations but because it was the only thing on the country's one television channel. And it was music. By this time I'd been to see a lot of live bands. Some were great, others grim. Distinguishing between the two was how I'd begun to establish my own tastes and a sense of who I was. The bands I liked operated, for the most part, on a subterranean level. They didn't consciously shun the world of radio, television and pop charts, but mass exposure was not uppermost in their thoughts. Space Waltz represented, if not quite the end of the world I had come to feel a part of at the Union Hall, then a distinct alternative. Glam rock had grown out of the music I loved but it had shed the idealism. This music sought the spotlight. It craved success and fame.

Forty years after first seeing Alastair Riddell on the family TV set, I am standing in his living room in Titirangi, Auckland. His house is tucked at the end of a leafy cul-de-sac, right next door to where he grew up. After his wife Vanessa greets me, Alastair emerges from a studio where he has been editing a feature film he has directed; it was written and produced by Vanessa, who is also the star.

There is a busy hum of creativity. A friend sits at the kitchen table tapping on a laptop, looking up at one point to pass an authoritative comment on a cultish British music festival. These days Alastair's hair is short. He wears jeans and a plain shirt. He does not wear make-up. He says he has been trying without success to get the *Herald* to give his film, *Broken Hallelujah*, some coverage. 'There was a time,' he says with a sigh, 'when "Alastair Riddell Makes Movie" would have been an instant headline.'

Regrettably, I have not come to ask about the film. I want to hear how he remembers the change I observed in my teens, when glam rock supplanted what could be broadly called blues rock. I have heard from other musicians that Alastair had started out as an aspiring bluesman.

He confirms this. 'The first two or three records I ever owned weren't pop records,' he says. 'They were black blues music, which I think my parents thought was quite good because they were very concerned about civil rights in America and the history of all that.'

Alastair's parents were part of Titirangi's bohemian community, which included actors, painters and potters. 'Don't be a conformist,' his mother advised him. 'People who achieve things are not conformists.'

The first record he bought, aged eight, was an LP by the eminent American folk blues artist Leadbelly. This was in 1960, before The Rolling Stones, The Animals and other British bands had spurred interest in the music. He loved it, and followed it with another blues album, this time by Josh White.

As a thirteen-year-old, Alastair would bus into Auckland on a Friday night to see The La De Da's play at The Galaxie, an alcohol-free dance club in Mount Eden. The La De Da's based their music on the blues-influenced sounds of the British groups, and had a national hit with 'How Is the Air Up There?', a cover of a song by an obscure American garage band that had all the snap and snarl of a great Stones' single.

If The La De Da's weren't on, Alastair might catch The Underdogs with their resident guitar hero Harvey Mann, or The Action, fronted by sandpaper-voiced Evan Silva. He clearly separates these bands, with their roots in rhythm and blues, from the psychedelia that had already become commercialised and infiltrated the airwaves. 'I liked the *real* psychedelia,' he says. 'I liked "I Am the Walrus". I didn't like twee songs about flowers.'

By the time The La De Da's left for Australia in 1967, white blues had gone global. Its unofficial spokesman was the British musician John Mayall, who styled himself as a campaigner for the blues in the manner of a political activist. His 1967 album *Crusade* was adorned with photos of Mayall and his band The Bluesbreakers brandishing placards as though they were at a protest march, with slogans like 'The Blues Needs Your Support'. 'I'm gonna fight for you J.B.', Mayall sang. J.B. was the late Mississippi bluesman J.B. Lenoir; in Mayall's song he seemed more like a martyred leader.

John Mayall's Bluesbreakers never had a hit single but the band became known as a musical hothouse, generating exceptional musicians such as Eric Clapton and Jack Bruce of Cream, Peter Green, John McVie and Mick Fleetwood of Fleetwood Mac, Mick Taylor of The Rolling Stones, and Andy Fraser of Free. Using the blues as a springboard, these groups developed individual rock styles that defied the three-minute limit of pop radio, and brought the guitar virtuoso into the spotlight.

New Zealand blues fans could be as earnest and zealous as any. Liking the blues meant, by implication, that you disliked a lot of other things – commercial music for a start. It distinguished you from the multitudes who accepted unquestioningly what they were fed by the radio. Blues fans argued passionately over obscure issues. Was the rural blues of Mississippi superior to the electrified urban blues of Chicago? Was the saxophone a legitimate blues instrument? Could white men play the blues?

They formed societies, held conventions. In December 1968

with his friend Selwyn Jones, Alastair Riddell organised the first National Blues Convention at Moller's Farm in West Auckland, a one-day event featuring various Auckland outfits, among them Original Sun Blues Band, which Alastair had formed with his older brother Ron. A second convention the following year built on the success of the first, spanning a full weekend and attracting performers and crowds from all over the country.

With their outspoken rejection of the commercial world, the blues fans were a natural fit with the burgeoning hippie movement. In fact, the 1969 convention seemed to double as an early gathering of the counterculture. Its alternative name Electric Picnic, the one printed on the ticket, had a decidedly psychedelic ring, and a programme note by organisers Riddell and Jones expressed the hope 'all those interested in the music and all the performers who concentrate on different fields of blues [would] combine in one great fantasmagorical hugglemaflop'.

Among the performers were the Mad Dog Jug Jook and Washboard Band, led by multi-instrumentalist Robbie Laven and featuring future Windy City Struggler Andrew Delahunty on harmonica, and a young Auckland jug band called The Greasy Handful, whose singer, Graham Brazier, would make his name six years later with Hello Sailor. Rick Bryant, up from Wellington, sang with at least three groups that weekend: the electric blues band Gutbucket; The Windy City Strugglers and a band of his own, Rick and The Rockets, that stretched the definition of blues to its cosmic limits.

Among the Rockets' line-up, which was seldom consistent from one gig to the next, were guitarists Graeme Nesbitt and Peter Kennedy. Their repertoire was dictated by a sense of the absurd, heightened by a shared enthusiasm for controlled substances. Highlights of their Moller's Farm set included an arrangement of 'The Teddy Bears' Picnic', a convincing cover of The Goons' 'Ying Tong Song', and a revival of 'Running Bear', the 1960 Johnny Preston hit with its tale of star-crossed Native American lovers and a politically unsound quasi-ethnic chorus. Alastair Riddell grins when I remind him of Rick and The Rockets. 'They were hilarious, one of the highlights of the show,' he says. 'Peter Kennedy did the best Bluebottle I ever heard.'

Giving themselves a name in the '50s tradition of Johnny Devlin and The Devils and Max Merritt and The Meteors, at a time when the fashion was for abstract or surrealistic handles such as Fresh Air and Throb, was just part of Rick and The Rockets' subversiveness. But the band was definitely psychedelic.

Rick Bryant remembers hearing an entire paddock-full of festival-goers laughing as one. The whole event was 'very unusual. Several thousand people were having their first weekend as hippies. A lot of people were having their first LSD trips. A *lot*. Hundreds and hundreds.

'There were specs going round where the lenses were pyramids and colours. It was like wearing an acid trip: "Here, have a trip with your trip." It was a very pleasant occasion, a micro Woodstock, entirely pacific. There was nobody drunk or ugly, just a lot of fairly innocent young people being harmless and out of it.'

By the time the '70s rolled around, Alastair Riddell was losing interest in the blues. The music was so deeply rooted in the African-American experience, how could it ever be an authentic vehicle for a middle-class intellectual in New Zealand? He was seeing possibilities in some of the new music coming out of Britain – initially the 'progressive' rock of groups such as King Crimson and Van Der Graaf Generator, then the more theatricalised pop of David Bowie and Roxy Music. He was also listening to songwriters from outside the rock realm, among them the French chanteur Jacques Brel and the English actor and satirist Anthony Newley.

As Wellington's Rick and The Rockets evolved into Mammal, up in Auckland Riddell formed Orb with Peter Cuddihy, Tony Raynor, Wally Wilkinson and Paul Crowther. Like Mammal, Orb was essentially a university band. It spiced its sets of covers with Riddell originals, including 'Sea Bird', which would reappear in the repertoire of Riddell's later group, Space Waltz. It became one of the first New Zealand bands to feature a synthesiser, which was constructed by drummer and electronics boffin Crowther.

In between Orb and Space Waltz, Riddell would cannily form another band, Stuart and The Belmonts. Satirically named for Brian Stuart, head of the Auckland vice squad, and the Holden Belmont cars driven by the New Zealand police force, it was a covers band devised with the express purpose of providing a living, and perhaps subsidising some of Riddell's more creative projects. From 1972 to '74 Riddell – with The Belmonts, which included Raynor, Steve Hughes, Greg Clark and Brent Eccles – worked two or three nights a week at weddings, twenty-firsts and RSA clubs, playing popular favourites from Harry Belafonte to Elton John. They even played Lion Breweries' booze barns until Richard Holden fired them for allegedly stealing beer.

If Stuart and The Belmonts was Alastair Riddell's concession to the musical tastes of middle New Zealand, Space Waltz was a ploy to ambush it with his own. And at least for a short time it worked. The notion of glam rock had been seeping into the country since the early '70s, with the hit singles of T. Rex and its glitter-and-satin star Marc Bolan. It had been consolidated in the person of David Bowie, who was fast emerging as the most significant English pop star of the decade. Although it had the same blues roots as every kind of rock since Elvis Presley, glam put no premium on authenticity. It was a shameless game of dress-ups, reviving the styles and fashions of early rock 'n' roll. Faded denim was out; satins and leopard skins were back. There were touches of sexual ambiguity and apocalyptic angst. Songs tended to be punchy and concise: your fifteen-minute guitar solos will no longer be required, Mr Clapton.

Riddell was characterised as a local version of Bowie, then known for the gender-bending personae of Ziggy Stardust and Aladdin Sane. Although the similarities were undeniable, 'David Bowie never wrote a song even vaguely like "Out on the Street"', Alastair points out. 'It has a swing chorus and a half-time verse. Jacques Brel and Peter Hamill were at least as big an influence on me, but in New Zealand all anybody could ever hear was Bowie. He was the only reference point we had.'

'Out on the Street' might have been the beginning of a sustained career but EMI, the company that had signed Riddell, had no idea what to do with him. For a follow-up, one staff member suggested he try and write something like songs by the Canadian classic rock group Bachman-Turner Overdrive. Alastair remembers, 'Before it happened I had this pure vision

about who I was and what I wanted to do. By the time I'd been in EMI's thrall for three or four months I was absolutely losing my way. My energy just completely dissipated.'

Riddell ventured to Australia, where a Melbourne music manager, Michael Browning, had shown interest in Space Waltz. Browning proposed taking the band to Britain, along with another he had just signed, AC/DC. Riddell was keen but couldn't reach consensus with the other band members. By the time the Space Waltz album came out in 1975, Tony Raynor, Wally Wilkinson and Paul Crowther had left to join Split Enz. The glam moment was almost over. Its absorption into the mainstream could be seen in the multitude of pub covers bands around New Zealand that had adopted a glam look.

Yet, emerging from the university blues and psychedelic scene, Space Waltz had left a legacy: it had showed a way out of the underground and towards success and fame. In May 1975, at the height of its popularity, it had headlined a concert at the Auckland Town Hall. In the music magazine *Hot Licks*, reviewer Roger Muir had observed: 'It looks like another one of those visiting rock concerts, judging by the crowd ... Hey – two local groups, would you believe. Things must be looking up for the local music scene at last.'

Opening the show was a band that had done its time on the university circuit, played clubs and even pubs, and was now looking to realise much bigger dreams.

11
A DRAGON'S TALE

A siren's oscillation cuts through the Christchurch night. You can't tell where the sound is coming from until a Ford Transit van rounds the corner with a police car in pursuit, lights strobing madly. Behind the wheel of the van is a man dressed in red and pink lycra, with shoulder-length hair and mascara. But it's the one in the passenger seat the cops are after.

But I'm getting ahead of myself.

Most of what I know about these events I've learned only lately, from a man I had never previously met or spoken with. It was October 2014 when Ray Goodwin, a guitarist and founder member of Dragon, emailed me. He was in an isolated region of New South Wales known as Northern Rivers. His nearest town was Mullumbimby, where he went for cellphone service and wi-fi. Somehow word had reached him that I was writing about Graeme Nesbitt and memories had stirred. He wanted me to know he would be happy to help.

I emailed back, thanking him for his offer and wondering when he might be free to answer some questions. I never had to ask any questions: the memories began flowing to my inbox almost immediately, a trickle at first, then a torrent.

Goodwin remembers first meeting Graeme Nesbitt in 1971 at a Student Arts Festival in Palmerston North, where Nesbitt was one of the organisers. Goodwin was down from Auckland with a band, OK Dinghy, which also included future Dragon mainstay Todd Hunter. He says Mammal were on the bill as well, but this may have been the final incarnation of Rick and The Rockets. If the details are hazy, he blames it on the thing for which the festival is best remembered: Black Sumatran pot. The drug had reportedly been smuggled into New Zealand by Aussie surfers, and was so powerful a joint could render ten people stupefied for hours. 'For years afterwards this pot was highly sought after but never turned up,' Goodwin adds wistfully.

Having had a glimpse of Nesbitt's entrepreneurial flare, Goodwin wrote to him asking for his help to lift the newly formed Dragon out of the Auckland circuit – which mostly revolved around a single club gig – and on to the national stage. He had been impressed by the way Graeme had put Mammal on the road, cultivating an audience centred on university campuses.

Nesbitt was not particularly taken with Dragon's style of music, a rather heavy-handed prog rock, but he saw in the group a touch of the professional ambition that Mammal – much as he loved them as people and musicians – lacked, sometimes to a comical degree. Mammal's mishaps were an endless source of amusement. Nesbitt would regale Goodwin with stories of band members getting 'stoned enough to play' then losing their way to the stage, or Rick Bryant, rendered insensible by Mandrax, trying to navigate one of his Jaguars down a narrow Thorndon

street, bouncing off every parked vehicle. An inveterate collector, Rick's obsession was clapped-out 1950s Jags. Most of the cars he hit were his own.

The members of Dragon were, by contrast, go-getters. At the centre of the group were the two brothers from Taumarunui, Todd and Marc Hunter. Marc was the singer. Todd, the elder of the two, played bass and was sober and responsible. Largely through his efforts, Dragon had already succeeded in wangling a recording deal with Polygram; the company would release their ponderous quasi-concept album *Universal Radio* in early 1973.

Goodwin remembers Graeme Nesbitt wondering out loud if Dragon might be able to incorporate some members of Mammal. Goodwin didn't believe such a merger could possibly work, unless as some sort of extended family, a Grateful Dead-style commune. Nesbitt, though, seemed to be thinking further ahead, and in a sense his vision would come true. Within four years Dragon would be the top band in Australasia, living a life of rock-star excess, with two of Mammal's star players in the line-up.

The first Mammal to sign up was guitarist Robert Taylor. Graeme Nesbitt hustled him into Dragon following Mammal's demise in late 1974, setting the group in a new, grittier direction. A couple of years later, he would similarly manoeuvre Mammal's Kerry Jacobsen into the Dragon drum seat.

Graeme's involvement with Dragon had begun straight after Goodwin's initial appeal, although no managerial role was ever formalised. He started building the band's profile in Wellington, at first co-billing them with Mammal at the Union Hall, and later giving them headline status at the much larger Town Hall. He negotiated their appearance in a cinema commercial for Pinky chocolate bars, in which Marc Hunter managed to make an innocuous jingle sound like a series of lurid double entendres. ('Take off your red satin wrapper,' he crooned.)

Graeme also accompanied Dragon to Fiji on an infamous 1974 tour, where he inadvertently became the star of the show. In a foreshadowing of their future hit 'April Sun in Cuba' – *Tired of the city life, summer on the run* – Dragon had hatched a plan to get out of Granny's, the downtown Auckland nightclub where they had been resident most of the year, and decamp to the tropics. Todd and Marc's mother Voy came from Rotuma, a small volcanic island near Fiji, and the brothers were keen to connect with family there. An uncle known as Fast Eddie, who ran a wedding reception lounge in Mangere, South Auckland, helped

them get a booking at the aptly named Golden Dragon nightclub in Suva. Graeme would accompany them as tour manager.

At the Golden Dragon the band was assigned a minder with the nickname Money. Money found them accommodation in a brothel run by a pair of Indian brothers who rented beds at two dollars per night. 'We discovered the meaning of his name two weeks later,' Goodwin later wrote in a tour journal published in *Hot Licks*, 'when we realised he'd managed to borrow at least ninety dollars from different members of the band without any sign of repayment.'

Graeme found a local doctor who would prescribe generous

amounts of Mandrax for insomnia and ephedrine for fatigue. This kept the party stoned for the duration of the visit, explaining the cryptic title of Goodwin's *Hot Licks* piece, 'Last Mandy in Nandi'. The band had stopped in Nadi, pronounced Nandi, for three days on the way home, although Goodwin made no mention of the drugs.

Like the club-goers of Auckland, Golden Dragon's clientele showed little interest in Dragon's original material so the band played the same tired covers as they had at Granny's, sharing the stage with Millie, a local drag queen who gave renditions of 'Lovely Hula Hands' in an operatic falsetto. When they were invited to play at a one-off event in a local hall, billed as *The 1st Suva Rock Concert*, band members were determined to air their original songs. The locals, though, were merely bemused by the prog rock. It was the opening act that received the standing ovation: in rented cowboy regalia, Nesbitt strummed an acoustic guitar and sang such country classics as 'Hey, Good Lookin'' and 'Blackboard of My Heart' to wild applause.

Graeme Nesbitt went on to produce one of the best records Dragon would ever make. 'Education' was a song of Robert Taylor's – a parting shot, perhaps, at the world of student rock (*talking to my brother, educated fool*) with a taut wiry guitar riff. It originally featured in the repertoire of Mammal, but once Robert joined Dragon Graeme picked it up as a single. With Robert singing lead, Marc Hunter was left to play congas, which Graeme lifted high in the mix to give the recording a funky, almost Little Feat feel. To Robert's chagrin, after he left the smoke-filled studio and went home, Graeme and whoever else was still around smoked another joint and decided the track sounded a bit slow. They sped up the tape for the final master. This may have enlivened the groove but it left Robert's vocal sounding, he would tell me when I interviewed him, 'like Joni Mitchell or a squirrel'.

In late 1974, Dragon toured New Zealand to promote the single. They had crossed Cook Strait and were en route to Christchurch when their main vehicle, a bus, blew its engine. To repair it would cost thousands of dollars, money they didn't have, but the cost of cancelling gigs in Christchurch and Dunedin would be even greater. Goodwin called Graeme, who came up with a solution: a bag full of buddha sticks.

Goodwin now believes Graeme's phone was being tapped. As soon as Graeme arrived in Christchurch with the contraband that could be sold to settle the group's debts, the police were on his tail. The arrest was dramatic. Goodwin, who had collected him from the airport in the band's Ford Transit, attempted to outrun the police and did so for several blocks. But before long he and Graeme were in Addington Prison, pending remand.

Goodwin emailed me: 'I was on my way to a gig, so wearing my red/pink ensemble with mascara of course, and had to endure stony stares from drooling inmates. But I had double helpings from the tranny Samoan giant cook! We were given protection cards by Mick the Murderer once it was established I could play some Rory Gallagher. Graeme and I used to meet every day in the exercise yard, or at church services, the only other time you could get out of the cell. His spirits were amazing. Boy, could he focus. He would have been a hero in the trenches or on the battlefield.'

Goodwin was ultimately discharged and Graeme took the rap. He was sentenced to two and a half years in prison. Goodwin recalled Graeme's sentencing: 'I still seek closure on Graeme. I have carried such angst scars since our bust in 74. What a drag …'

He remembers the high times that preceded the fall: 'Graeme was tripping the light fantastic … he loved the nerve/success factor thing … the bux meant zilch. He would take a dozen people to the best restaurant and pick up the tab, these are povo line musos etc. who normally lived on diets of brown rice, burgers and spuds … He kind of attempted to infuse them all with a sense of style/taste. His farewell do at Macavity's in Wellington was a screech … Porn was screened, a kind of belated acid test with acid replaced by champers, buddha and good wine, the kitchen staff and others all hitting up speed balls in the dunnies … Now Graeme is haunting me in a very affable way.'

12
DEPARTURES

At the end of 1974, aged sixteen, I sat my University Entrance exams, and without waiting for the results left school. A couple of weeks before Christmas my friend Dave and I went for a walk by the railway yards and within an hour we had jobs loading goods trains. Dave had been staying with us since school finished: he preferred my family to his own. All he would say about his home life was that his father worked in a bank and hated music. Now that Dave had an income he was planning to get a flat with a few of our friends. I could move in too if I liked.

The flat was halfway up a steep hill from the city and ten minutes' walk from the house in North Terrace where I had grown up and the rest of the family still lived. I figured I could always go home if I wanted. The rent was twenty dollars. Each week one of us would take it to the old copper-domed building on Lambton Quay that was the Public Trust Office and hand it to a teller seated behind a polished wooden counter.

Five of us lived in the flat. As well as Dave and me, there were Hank, Matt and Michael. Hank was the first to have a girlfriend stay the night. Her name was Angela and I was in love with her. I had been ever since the first day she walked into our sixth form French class and so had half the other boys in the room. Angela wore black velvet jeans and had quick dark eyes. Her family had recently shifted from Auckland and she already had a boyfriend in the seventh form, a fey aesthete with a ponytail and a hand-knitted cap whom I hated on sight. It turned out she was interested in music. She said she and her boyfriend had some good records, which gave me something to talk to her about.

One night I went to a party with a few friends and Angela was there. There was no sign of the boyfriend. She was just starting to tell me how they'd broken up when some older guys, ex-Onslow, appeared. I may as well have been invisible; they reeled towards her, asking with whisky breath what she was doing that night and who she was with. At that moment Angela and I took a half-step towards each other, my arm wrapping around her shoulder. She gently leaned in. For the first time the drunks noticed me and realised they had seen me before. 'Is she your girlfriend?' 'Are you going out with her?' they asked in mocking, incredulous tones. Then to Angela, 'Are you with *that* guy?' I don't remember either of us replying. Nor could I figure out what to say to Angela after the men had stumbled off to test their charms on other women. I let go of her, but held on to the moment.

Over the next few months I would see Angela, but only at school or parties. Although a few couples had formed within my circle of friends, mostly we moved in a pack. We'd hear of a party somewhere, or someone's parents would be away for the weekend, and a dozen of us would find our way there by train or on foot. Enough money would be scraped together to buy a carafe of wine.

One night there was going be a Van Morrison concert on TV. Angela's parents were out so we all repaired to her place to drink wine and watch Van. I'd been listening obsessively to *Astral Weeks* and staring endlessly at the double-exposed image on the cover. This had led me to envisage Van as a romantic dashing poet with flowing hair, so I was unprepared for what appeared on the screen. The man clutching the microphone and intoning those intense and mysterious incantations was short, slightly stout, and looked somewhat grouchy. He reminded me of Rick Bryant.

After the programme we drank more wine, a few people rolled cigarettes, and Angela put on *Court and Spark*, a record she had just bought. I hadn't heard much Joni Mitchell before. I thought of her as one of those strummy folk singers and had filed her as 'wet', along with James Taylor. But this was different. There were horns and harmonies and skittering jazzy rhythms. The chords formed intricate pictures, and so did the words. Joni sang about love and its complications. There seemed to be a lot of men trailing through her songs, all offering her things. She wondered whether she really wanted any of the men. She was independent and strong, yet confessed to insecurities. In my mind, Angela and the voice in those Joni Mitchell songs became one.

Before long Angela was going out with Hank. A few months passed and Hank's parents offered him a trip to Europe, so I moved into his room, which was bigger than mine. He had left a box of stuff behind, among it spare guitar strings, a copy of Greil Marcus's *Mystery Train* and a packet of condoms.

One night Angela came around. It was already late and before long everyone else had gone to bed. We talked and I went to put on some music. I'd decided to play *Blood on the Tracks*, Bob Dylan's new album. I'd been a Dylan fan since school and loved *Highway 61 Revisited* and *Blonde on Blonde*, but his recent albums had seemed strangely toothless. This new record, though, showed him rejuvenated, aching and raging with love for someone beyond his reach.

I was close to dropping the tone arm on 'Tangled Up in Blue' when it occurred to me that Dylan's rage might be a bit much for the quiet intimacy of the occasion. I opted instead for a Phoebe Snow record I knew Angela liked. Eventually I asked where she was staying the night and she said she guessed in Hank's room. If she felt any guilt about sharing her boyfriend's old bed with me she didn't say so, and she laughed when I got up to rummage in the dark through his box of ephemera for the condoms.

Not long after that I got a letter from Hank. He was having a good time, he said. Parties in England were just the same as in New Zealand: someone always ended up playing *Exile on Main Street*. He'd bought new albums by Grateful Dead and Bonnie Raitt and thought I'd like them. He also said something cryptic about watching out for naked women in his old room. I still wasn't sure Angela and I were actually going out though, and she seemed to prefer it that way. I'd ring her at home and her mother would say she had gone away for the weekend, she didn't know where. A line from *Court and Spark* went through my head: *We love our loving, but not like we love our freedom.*

In our flat in the middle of winter you got out of bed only when you had to. Dave left before dawn, walking down the hill to the mess of mud and concrete where he was now employed as a labourer on construction of the new motorway. Matt and I had also worked there until the foreman caught us leaning on our shovels. He fired us but that was okay: the eighty dollars in my final pay packet could keep me going for a couple of months.

One morning at around 8.30, Matt's sister, down from Coromandel with her incense and crunchy granola, burst into my room and woke me. 'I'm sorry Nick, but there's a girl on the phone who says she needs to talk to you. She sounds a bit upset.' It was my fourteen-year-old sister Thomasin. Her voice was very clear and she was speaking in short sentences which seemed to shatter as soon as they left the receiver. *Dad has died. He's had a heart attack and died. Just now. Mum's not here. You have to come.* I was trying to put her words back together in some way that made sense as I stepped out the door. I think somebody called to me, 'Is everything okay?' and I might have answered, 'I don't think so' but it's hard to know whether any words came out. I felt like I was moving and frozen at the same time.

When I got to the house the front door was hanging open, as though someone had just left. Thomasin and my younger brother Tim were waiting for me in the hallway. Dad had woken them in the night in pain. They had sat with him as he lay in bed. He told them he thought it was his heart. By early morning he was worse and asked them to call the doctor. Mum was away and they hadn't been able to get hold of her.

I don't know how long we stood there, three confused kids, or how much time elapsed before I went into the bedroom. I had no idea what I'd find but I didn't expect to see a doctor leaning over the bed. I could see my father's shoulder and his silvery hair, but the doctor hadn't seen me and I didn't want to startle him so I backed silently out of the room. One of us must have rung Dennis, a family friend, because before long he was there. Mum turned up after that.

The last time I had seen Dad had been about a week before. I'd popped home for some reason. We hadn't talked for long. He might have asked if I was happy, I'm not sure. What I remember was his asking whether I noticed anything different about him? I looked. I could see his hair had grown greyer and he hadn't been to the barber for a while. But that wasn't it. Same horn-rimmed glasses, gentle blue jersey.

'I don't know,' I said.

'I've given up smoking.' The pipe he had puffed on almost constantly for as long as I could remember had gone.

'Was that hard to do?' I asked, surprised. I knew how addictive tobacco was supposed to be, and had listened to some of my mates, sixteen, seventeen years old, grumbling like codgers about their nicotine habits as they licked their papers and rummaged in their packets of Drum.

He thought about it for a moment. 'No,' he said softly. I didn't ask any more questions.

Over the next couple of days a lot of decisions were made and I had nothing to do with any of them. If my father could be alive one moment and dead the next, what could I do that would possibly make any difference to anything anyway? Someone from the university organised a memorial service. It was held in the Union Hall. A lot of Dad's friends and colleagues made speeches. Mum didn't speak. Nor did any of us kids. I don't think anyone even asked us.

That night there was a dance at Onslow, the school I had left six months before. Our band, which had acquired the name Last Gasp, had been booked to play. I remember someone asking if I still wanted to do it, having just lost my dad and all that. I couldn't really say. This was all new territory. I don't recall what we played that night, but I remember a crowd of friends showing up and dancing in front of the stage. At the end of the first set some of the band went outside for a cigarette but Angela grabbed my hand and took me to her family's house, ten minutes away. Her parents must have seen me as I walked past the living room where they were watching television but they didn't say anything. I followed her to her room. She closed the door and led me urgently to her bed.

I remember that later, when our band had played its last set and the gear was packed away, Thomasin and lots of her friends and most of my flatmates went to someone's parents' place and drank ginger wine on the lawn in the dark, and somebody asked if this was a wake. Whisky was drunk, people were laughing and a few were being sick. I recall looking across the garden and seeing Dave sitting on his own. He looked like the saddest person I'd ever seen. Perhaps he sensed that with the loss of my father things were going to change at our home, which had been his refuge. If I could have seen myself, what would I have looked like? A boy stunned by grief, or giddy with sex and rock 'n' roll?

My father's death at forty-six was so sudden and unexpected it was as though a meteorite had crashed into our family. Where Con had stood there was now a crater. We, the survivors, picked ourselves up, slightly stunned, looked at each other, and as we had no visible injuries did our best to carry on.

I can only imagine how my mother felt about not being at home the night Thomasin and Tim sat with our father as he lay dying. For her, the shock and loss were as great as for the rest of us, but there had been many nights over the previous five years that she hadn't been home. She had a lover an hour's drive up the coast, and sometimes spent a night or weekend with him. We all knew this, and Con seemed to accept it, if sadly. There was never any suggestion that our parents would break up and I'm not sure they even considered it. They had a genuine love and admiration for each other, and the family at North Terrace was at its heart nuclear and functional. At some point Mum said to me casually but with a note of relief that she thought Dad might have a girlfriend. I believe he had several in those last years, although he never introduced them to us and never seemed far from home.

A few months after my father died, my mother moved up the coast to live with her lover, Graham Cooper, taking Tim and our foster brother Tom with her. Graham would provide them with stability and a new home. Thomasin, who was still at school, stayed on at North Terrace and I moved back there to live with her and an assortment of our friends.

The big old villa was transformed from a family home into a teenage flat. It wasn't always easy to tell who was living there and who was just passing by. Sally, a girl whom Thomasin and I had known since we were kids, had recently finished school and she moved in with us. Thomasin started going out with a guy who rode a motorbike, had a large jar of unidentified pills that he had obtained during his job driving a chemist's van and slept with a knife under his pillow. He moved in too. Another room was occupied by a quiet painter who would toil for days and nights behind the closed door. If it hadn't been for the smell of turps and oil we'd have had no idea what he was up to. Occasionally he'd emerge with a fresh artwork and hang it on the living-room wall. Then he'd get drunk, decide the painting was no good, tear it off the wall and destroy it. The next day he would look sadly at the remains and become stricken with remorse, which was usually the cue for getting drunk again.

Sometimes I'd wake up to find a stranger crashed out on the couch, or a guest making breakfast in the kitchen, or someone smoking hash over the stove. There were parties fuelled by pot and carafes of cheap wine. *Exile on Main Street* was on the stereo a lot. It was a life of freedom most teenagers could only fantasise about. My mother was working full-time at the Justice Department as well as looking after Tim, Tom and Graham, who was suffering from a long-term illness. Her life was difficult enough without having to keep an eye on us, but she seemed to have confidence in the ability of her children to make responsible decisions and steer their own lives.

Hank came back from overseas. Angela went back to him for a while, then back to me, then up north, where her parents had gone to start a macadamia farm. I turned seventeen and didn't really know what I was doing. Nor did I have anyone to advise me. Music seemed a good thing to hang on to.

Fairport
SPLIT ENZ
Wellington Opera House
Wed 2 July
BILL COSBY

13
THE WINDY CITY STRUGGLERS GO ELECTRIC

A few months after my father died I got a call from Bill Lake. His acoustic jug band The Windy City Strugglers had decided to add electric instruments and needed a bass player. Bob Dylan going electric in 1965 had changed the cultural course of the twentieth century. The Windy City Strugglers doing the same thing a decade later would have little impact other than a minor increase in someone's power bill, but it took me into the Royal Tiger Tavern.

The Strugglers had started in 1968, soon after Bill arrived in Wellington from Australia, his birthplace, which he had left to avoid being called up for Vietnam. Obsessed with the blues of the Mississippi delta – recordings from the 1920s and '30s that had begun to be reissued by folkloric labels such as Folkways and Arhoolie – he had taught himself to play guitar, harmonica and mandolin in this arcane style: wiry, nervy, quietly intense, rather like Bill himself.

Wellington already had its enclave of blues followers but most had come to the music via its English interpreters, of whom Eric Clapton was the most renowned. A few local sophisticates such as Colin Heath and Max Winnie knew the blues as a tributary of the folk and jazz they already played. But everyone who heard Bill instantly sensed an authenticity that was missing from the Clapton copyists. You could hear that his blues came from somewhere closer to the source. Even reissued records of early blues were hard to come by in New Zealand, and the original 78s were mythical, but Bill sounded almost as if he had stepped out of one of those shellac discs.

The Strugglers had made their name playing at folk and blues festivals. 'You've got that authentic shaky sound,' Max Winnie had enthused to Geoff Rashbrooke, the band's original mandolin and piano player, after their ramshackle debut at the 1968 Wellington Folk Festival. I had seen them at the Union Hall playing opening sets for Mammal. About half of Mammal seemed to be in the Strugglers as well. They would cluster centre stage, trying to aim their instruments in the general direction of whatever microphones were at hand. Bill's acoustic guitar usually lacked a strap so to play it he would stand slightly hunched, with the instrument balanced tenuously on his knee. Rick Bryant stood upright, eyes shut tightly in concentration as he flailed at a washboard, an adapted laundry tool he struck percussively with thimbled fingers, keeping it aloft by poking one of its pronged ends perilously down the front of his jeans.

By 1975 Bill's delta blues purism had relaxed a little. He had dabbled in rock with bands such as Original Sin and Mammal, and come to appreciate what American groups like The Band and Little Feat were doing, using the blues as a foundation for

contemporary songs. Adding electric guitars and bass to the Strugglers would give him a chance to explore similar territory, write his own material and get the group out of the folk clubs. Perhaps they could even earn a little money. The Strugglers at this point consisted of Bill, Geoff Rashbrooke, Andrew

Delahunty and Steve Hunt. Rick was not currently with the group: he was in Witako Prison, serving eighteen months for cannabis possession.

I had met Bill a few months earlier when a girl I knew from Onslow, older than me and at university, had brought him to a church hall where Last Gasp were playing out of tune to a few dozen friends. He had heard we did 'Rock 'n' Roll, Hoochie Koo'. Would we mind if he joined us for that song, and was there a guitar he could use? Our rhythm guitarist was quickly relegated to tambourine.

Now I was going to join Bill's band. I was still a few years away from being legally allowed into licensed premises, but Bill said he thought I'd be all right as long as I stayed away from the bar. And maybe I should keep my head down during the breaks. As for my bass playing, that was hardly going to threaten the Strugglers' authentic shakiness.

The first Windy City Strugglers' gig I played was at the Royal Tiger and had come via Bill's friend Midge Marsden. I had listened to Marsden's *Blues Is News* programme on the radio. His band, Country Flyers, had been packing out the tavern's lounge bar several nights a week for eighteen months. The Flyers had a line-up that included, at various times, a number of musicians I'd seen in the psychedelic rock shows at the Union Hall. Bass player Neil Hannan had been in Olibet, drummer Jim Lawrie in Highway and Bud Hooper – Lawrie's successor in the Flyers – in Billy T.K.'s Powerhouse. There was nothing psychedelic about the Flyers though. They played in the bare house lighting of the Tiger and their music was essentially country, a genre associated with the most conservative side of American culture. From the little I'd heard, country music's message seemed to be we don't smoke no marijuana, stand by your man, and it's America, love it or leave it. The typical country music fan was a shotgun-wielding redneck straight out of *Easy Rider*. But by the '70s, country's conservatism was being subverted by such American bands as The Byrds, Grateful Dead and The Flying Burrito Brothers, who parcelled up anti-establishment messages in songs that had the traditional melodies, high lonesome harmonies and clean twanging guitars of classic country.

The Flyers picked up on this style and gave it a local twist. They were all excellent musicians and Midge Marsden was a gracious, gregarious front man, but the star was a young left-handed guitarist called Richard Kennedy, who was seventeen when he joined the band in 1974. During the night he would perform several showstoppers. He localised the R&B standard 'It Should Have Been Me', changing the line about a bowl of chilli to a packet of fish and chips. And he gave a nod to New Zealand's rural sector by closing each set with a note-perfect picking of the theme from television's *Country Calendar*. The Flyers made the ultimate pub music: good-humoured, instantly familiar, simple in essence yet played by virtuosi.

By the end of 1975 the Flyers had become so popular the publican was complaining. The crowds made it almost impossible to get to the bar. Some nights standing room was at such a premium there were people hanging off the railings at the side of the stairs that led to the upstairs area where the bands performed. If the publican wanted entertainment that attracted fewer people, the Strugglers were just the band for the job.

The arrival of music at the Royal Tiger had coincided with the closure in 1973 of the Duke of Edinburgh, a hotel at the corner of Manners and Willis Streets that had through the '60s been the meeting place of Wellington's students, intellectuals and fringe-dwellers. If you were walking from the university into the city, taking a shortcut down the precipitous Allenby Terrace steps to emerge from the gothic shadow of St Mary of the Angels, the Duke was right in front of you, and once inside it could be hard to leave.

The Duke never had music but musicians often drank there. It was the setting of a pivotal scene in the 1969 film *Tank Busters*, in which an assortment of students, dropouts, criminals and musicians – typical Duke dwellers in other words – discussed the viability of robbing a safe at the university. The film was directed by future Blerta member Geoff Murphy and marked the feature film debut of Bruno Lawrence. Like Rick Bryant and Bill Lake, Lawrence and Murphy were regulars at the Duke. It was a place where drugs, mainly pot and acid, could be bought. James K. Baxter would wander in with a poem or a sermon. Rick was introduced there to the famed British author Anthony Burgess, and to the controversial Scottish psychiatrist R.D. Laing.

With the Duke empty and awaiting demolition, some of the regulars had migrated to the Royal Tiger. Opened in 1971 and trumpeted by Lion Breweries as another triumph of its architectural department, the concrete-block and timber-beam tavern soon acquired an atmosphere of lawlessness, like a saloon on the edge of the Wild West. It consisted of two bars – a lounge and a public bar – and a bottle store. While the lounge was colonised by Duke refugees and other bohemians, the public bar became the haunt of bikers and gang members. Entrances to the two bars were on opposite sides of the building. However, the two clienteles, each in their own way outlaws from mainstream society, shared the toilets. Patched gang members and student hippies would find themselves eyeball to eyeball in the narrow corridor, or standing next to each other at the urinals. Both bars saw the occasional altercation. One night, when Bill Lake had been sitting in with the Flyers, a fight broke out. Someone grabbed Bill's Stratocaster – whether as a shield or weapon it was hard to tell – and by the time Bill retrieved it the instrument was a splintered wreck. However, there was never any conflict reported between the two distinct subcultures that occupied the respective bars.

At the end of 1975 Robert Muldoon, a hard-line conservative, was elected prime minister and immediately began pushing new legislation that would increase police powers, particularly to break up gatherings of gangs. His attitude to the emerging Māori protest movement was dismissive and his approach to race relations insensitive, but in 1976 he agreed to meet with members of Black Power. Some commentators believed he was looking for genuine solutions to gang violence and unemployment. Others have suggested he had fantasies of cultivating a private army.

The venue was the public bar of the Royal Tiger. Between twenty and thirty Black Power members showed up. Sociologist Jarrod Gilbert has suggested that 'Muldoon being a short man, it is possible the hotel's management did not know the prime minister was present because members of the gang obscured him.' Whether this is true, it is recorded that the management stopped serving alcohol and called the cops, who didn't believe the prime minister was present until he emerged from the pack and asked them what they wanted. 'Despite the fact that the group was causing no trouble,' Gilbert writes, 'Muldoon and the Black Power members moved on from the tavern and adjourned to a gang address to finish their discussion and drinks.'

If they had been looking for illegal activities, the police would have had more luck in the vicinity of the lounge bar. The punters there did not necessarily favour beer as their intoxicant of choice. Many arrived stoned and were content to dampen their droughty mouths with orange juice, drifting out to one of the nearby alleyways between sets for a few more lungfuls.

Marijuana was now easy to come by but what had once been shared, given away or sold for minimal profit by evangelists such as Graeme Nesbitt was becoming a lucrative business. One of my flatmates discovered a dairy halfway between our flat and the university where, if you knew the appropriate password, the cashier would sell you what looked like fossilised kebabs from under the counter. These buddha sticks were two-millimetre packets of dried marijuana buds wrapped around a bamboo skewer. We didn't yet know they were being imported from Thailand by a syndicate of New Zealand-based cannabis dealers, soon to be christened by the media the 'Mr Asia Drug Ring'.

The syndicate was moving into harder drugs, and you didn't have to look far to see the results. A regular at the Tiger was a guy a few years older than me. Pale and thin with long dark hair, he usually sat alone at a corner table. Someone called him Neil. I thought he looked a bit like The Rolling Stones' Keith Richards and admired his gift for stillness. He would stare intently at the edge of his table, sometimes for an entire set, as though there was a performance going on there that only he could see. One day I heard he had been found slumped in another bar, dead of a heroin overdose.

It was around this time, too, that I last saw Bruce, with whom I had consorted in Onslow's Glass Box. He came into the Tiger one night with a group of mates, noticed me on the bandstand, and gave me a nod and a wicked grin. A few weeks later I heard that he too had overdosed and died.

The lounge bar of the Tiger had two sections: a downstairs area that you entered from the street, and a mezzanine with its own bar, which was reached via an internal staircase. Bands usually played on the mezzanine but the Strugglers never got further than the bottom of the stairs. Unlike the rest of us, Geoff, a stubborn traditionalist, had refused to go electric so our gear included a steel-framed upright piano, slightly out of tune and very heavy. None of us was particularly practical or physically robust, and we endured such anguish getting the instrument into a van in Kelburn and then across town to the Tiger that, after stopping for breath just inside the doors of the lounge bar, we couldn't summon the strength to lift it again. We simply set up the rest of our rickety equipment around it.

As it turned out, our piano-moving marathon had been pretty much a waste of time, as the acoustic keyboard could barely be heard above the amplified guitars. One night, though, downtown Wellington was hit with a power outage. As the Tiger plunged into darkness the only thing audible was the tinkling of Geoff's piano keys.

DRAGON
& RED HOT PEPPERS
Sunday Nov. 14 .8pm
Wellington Town Hall
book at the D.I.C.

14
BROADER THEATRE

Wellington Town Hall, Sunday, November 14, 1976. This is where the big names play. It's where Igor Stravinsky conducted the Symphony Orchestra in 1961; where – before I was old enough, although I longed to be there – Wellington teenagers screamed and cried for The Beatles. It is where, in my thirteenth year, I studied B.B. King as he caressed Lucille, his Gibson 335 guitar, and preached his elegant blues, and where, more recently, Stewart Macpherson, a concert promoter, blocked a side entrance and ordered me to get out and stay out, after I almost succeeded in slipping through without a ticket to see Lou Reed. It is where on my eighteenth birthday I'd sat in the balcony, gazing down in wonder as Lowell George rode a silver train of slide guitar over the southern railway rhythms of his band Little Feat.

Local bands don't often play in this hall but tonight is a special occasion. Dragon have returned from Australia for a single concert. It's strange that their only New Zealand show is in Wellington. Back when they were still based in this country they were considered an Auckland band. But tonight is a strange night. Graeme Nesbitt is just out of jail and has brought back to his hometown the band he had been trying to help when he obtained the drugs that led to his imprisonment. In the two years he has been inside a lot has changed. After he was put away, Dragon went to Australia. Perhaps if he had been around they would have heeded his advice: consolidate your New Zealand success, pay your debts and go to Europe, where a German record label has shown interest. Instead they found themselves in the sleaze pits of Sydney's Kings Cross under the dubious influence of Greg Ollard, whom Graeme had known when they were both selling grass in Wellington but who was by then a major heroin supplier. Ollard hung around, slipping the band cash and smack.

Entering the bright foyer of the Town Hall on this Sunday night, I know little if any of this. I've just seen the posters around town advertising Dragon's return and am curious to see what a year and a half in Australia has done to the band. It's a long time since I last heard Robert Taylor, the wonderful guitarist I used to catch often with Mammal. He is now Dragon's star musician. Just a few weeks ago Kerry Jacobson, another ex-Mammal, flew in to join him. There was a dark reason behind Kerry's sudden recruitment: Dragon's drummer, Neil Storey, had died of a heroin overdose.

The audience in the Town Hall is seated as if for a classical recital, which suits the opening act, Red Hot Peppers, a band of Auckland musicians with whom Graeme has had a long association. They have recently released an album, a rare achievement for a New Zealand group, and it's lifted their profile. Their leader is Robbie Laven, a bearded, unsmiling figure who surrounds himself with instruments – flutes, mandolins, saxophones, guitars – all of which he plays at least competently and some spectacularly. I had seen him in 1972 at the Union Hall in a very different setting – with a rock 'n' roll revival act called 1953 Memorial Society Rock 'n' Roll Band. The highlight that night had been a version of 'Leader of the Pack', during which Rob Nesbitt had ridden a motorcycle on to the stage and revved it loudly during the choruses. This evening's performance is more sedate. The Peppers shuffle between swingy jazz tunes, bluesy numbers and country rock. Laven's constant switching of instruments – often several times within a single song – is entertaining but the music is polite, never rocking hard or getting loud. It seems to lull the audience into a TV-style stupor.

After this there is an interval. Cigarettes are smoked in the foyer. It's a cool crowd, lots of hair and denim. There are a few folkies who remember Laven and Taylor from university days. I see some familiar faces from the Royal Tiger, others from the Union Hall. I recognise Rod Bryant, Rick's brother, who used to play harmonica in bands with Rick. He sometimes helps Graeme with gigs but has a day job as a journalist. Rick isn't here – he's still in prison. He was caught with a pound of cannabis, so he was done for dealing, although people who knew him said he could easily have smoked that much on his own.

I run into Bill Lake and he has some news. He has just been talking to Robbie Laven, who has asked him to join the Red Hot Peppers. They have a tour booked and it will continue well into the New Year. This means regular work and a weekly wage. I offer encouragement, although it will mean the end of the Strugglers, at least for now.

During the intermission, Laven's arsenal of instruments is removed from the stage and replaced with a stark set of amplifiers, a simple electric piano and a drum kit on a high riser. The house lights fade to black. There's a flurry of movement on the darkened stage and with a crashing chord the scene is suddenly bathed in bright light. The five-headed Dragon is in front of us, breathing fire.

There is so much to take in that my senses go into shock. The music is extraordinarily loud. I recognise none of the songs. They seem so short there is hardly time to absorb their melodies, and each runs into the next without a pause. There is a physical power I've not witnessed before in any band, and the five musicians wield it like a weapon. But the most alarming thing is the way they look. Four of them – Robert Taylor, the Hunter brothers and pianist Paul Hewson – form an almost military row along the front of the stage. All are naturally tall and their height is exaggerated by the Cuban-heeled boots on which they totter precariously, as though the music is the only thing holding them up. They are rail thin.

At the back, on the riser, sits Kerry Jacobson. It is at most a couple of months since I last saw him playing Bee Gees and Average White Band covers with Tapestry in a Wellington nightclub, his main gig since the breakup of Mammal, but in the meantime he has been transformed almost beyond recognition. His hair has been bleached and dyed electric orange, razored short at the sides and styled into spikes. He looks like a sickly kid brother of Ziggy Stardust. And like the others he has lost weight. These are not the ponderous prog-rockers with their long pretentious songs I used to hear at the Union Hall. Their new songs are as lean as they are. They are unlike any New Zealand band I have ever seen.

Between songs Marc Hunter leers at the audience. They have a new album coming out soon, he says, and he hopes we like the songs we are hearing from it, although it is apparent from his sneering tone that he couldn't care less whether we do or not. He has a scarf tied around his skinny waist and sashays like a drag queen. At one point he produces a riding crop and waves it about, a sinister suggestion of an S&M act.

The pace lets up only once, for a new song called 'Sunshine'. In spite of its bright title, 'Sunshine' is a melancholy piece with a mournful chorus, which the four in the front line sing in powerful harmony. After maybe forty-five minutes on stage they launch into a furious finale of 'White Light/White Heat', Lou Reed's intravenous drug anthem, and then walk off. By now half the audience has already left, driven out by the merciless volume. Those still there mill about like stunned survivors of an accident. I look for Bill but he's nowhere to be found.

I'm not quite sure what I've just experienced, but as I walk with my flatmates back up the steps and zigzags to Kelburn I find myself saying, 'It looked like an advertisement for heroin.' I don't know what I mean. Maybe I'm repeating something I've heard someone else say. It just sounds right.

It is eighteen months before Dragon return again. By then they are the top band in Australia, with a string of hit singles. But their time at the top will be short-lived. Marc Hunter is fired when his addiction spirals out of control. In late 1984 Paul Hewson, the brilliant songwriter, quits and returns to New Zealand. A few weeks later he dies of an overdose.

Nearly forty years after that night I visit Rod Bryant at his home in the Wellington hills. We kneel on his living-room floor, surrounded by the contents of a cardboard box he has kept in his garage: photos, newspaper cuttings, press releases. There is a poster for the Town Hall concert. Does he remember it? 'Hell, yeah. Everyone was at that one. Cops. Terry Clark.' Clark would become infamous as the murderous ringleader of the Mr Asia syndicate, as documented in numerous books and television programmes. Back then, though, only people into drugs knew of him. In 1980 he was convicted in Britain for contracting the murder of Marty Johnstone, the dealer known as 'Mr Asia', with whom he had been in partnership. He died in Parkhurst Prison on the Isle of Wight in 1983, supposedly of natural causes. Clark is believed to have been responsible for the murders of up to a dozen members of the drug ring. One was Greg Ollard, Dragon's 'benefactor' from the band's early days in Sydney, who disappeared in 1978.

What was really going on that night? It wasn't just a concert, was it? Rod chuckles and shakes his head. 'No, it wasn't just a bloody concert, you're right.' He pauses and glances at a photograph staring up at us from among the paper clippings. Graeme is bright-eyed and smiling enigmatically, as if at some secret the rest of us are just figuring out. 'It was … broader theatre. It was Graeme saying, "Look at this. This is what we have created."'

Medley: 'Lawdy Miss Clawdy'/'Sunshine'

Johnny Devlin was New Zealand's first rock 'n' roll star. From 1958 he gave Kiwi teenagers their own surrogate Elvis. They came to his shows and screamed. His band were the Devils, and he was the Satin Satan. The fans tore the blue satin shirt from his back.

Johnny came from Gonville, a name that seemed to echo Elvis Presley's plea at the start of his epochal 1954 recording 'Milkcow Blues Boogie' for his band to 'get real gone'. That Gonville is a working-class suburb on the edge of Whanganui takes nothing away from the rock 'n' roll poetry of its name, but I've always pictured it as Goneville, a different place entirely. It's where you come from if you're real gone. And perhaps it's where you go to when you're gone as well.

Hold it fellas, let's get real, real gone for a change, huh?

Johnny borrowed Elvis's entreaty to kick off his first record, 'Lawdy Miss Clawdy'. You can hear him mimicking Elvis's words with just a trace of a Kiwi accent. 'Lawdy Miss Clawdy' was written and recorded by a New Orleans singer, Lloyd Price, in 1952. Elvis released a cover in 1957. Johnny's version, recorded a year later, was effectively a cover of Elvis's cover, but it had a primitive power of its own. It wasn't cut in a commercial studio but in Jive Centre, an Auckland nightclub where Johnny held a residency, on home-made equipment. The sound is clattering and uncontrolled; the echo effect is said to have been achieved by placing a microphone in the toilet.

Like hundreds of early rock 'n' roll songs, 'Lawdy Miss Clawdy' relies on a triplet figure played on a piano, and this circles through a simple set of changes. Led by Cockney pianist Don Turner, Johnny's backing band starts out at a languid walk, but after the singer stops them to issue Elvis's command they relaunch at twice the speed. The musicians may be accomplished jazzers moonlighting as rockers but the sound they make is rough and exciting.

By the 1970s the piano triplet was an archaism, used mostly to evoke nostalgia. It featured prominently in Ringo Starr's hit cover of the old rock 'n' roll song 'You're Sixteen', and chimed through the soundtrack of the 1973 coming-of-age film *American Graffiti*. Frank Zappa's Mothers of Invention had made *Cruising with Ruben and the Jets*, a homage to '50s rock 'n' roll, with Zappa referring on the sleeve, with mocking affection, to 'redundant piano triplets'.

Those triplets are the building blocks of Paul Hewson's 'Sunshine', the title song from Dragon's 1977 album, their first Australian long-player. However, the mood captured is not a longing for the past. It's something more complicated than that, and sadder.

'Sunshine' starts out at roughly the same tempo as Devlin's 'Lawdy Miss Clawdy' – before he has exhorted the fellas to get gone – and maintains that slumberous pace right through to the fade. From the opening bars, which pianist Hewson plays alone, there is something working against the song's title. Though every four-bar measure contains twenty-four eighth-notes – the

standard triplet equation – the first two bars divide those triplets unevenly, so that bar one seems to be a beat short while the next bar has too many. It stumbles with grace.

Then there's the melody. Songs about sunshine are supposed

to sound sunny. Hum a few bars of 'You Are My Sunshine', 'Walking on Sunshine' or 'Here Comes the Sun' and compare them to this melancholy tune. This is a melody that forecasts rain.

The paradox deepens when Marc Hunter steps to the mic, and in a voice cracking with fatigue begins to sing Hewson's lyric: *I'm leaving Broadway, no day or night, just colours shining, shining down on me*. The lines suggest an ageing Judy Garland contemplating the falling curtain at the twilight of her career, only the Broadway in this song isn't Garland's Broadway in New York, New York, the city that never sleeps. It's the seedy corridor through inner-city Sydney where the members of Dragon lived, and one died, as they began their conquest of the Australian pop world.

There's a pause at the end of the verse before the rest of the band join Hunter in harmony for this strangely equivocal chorus:

I'm in the sunshine
I'm wasting time
I'm in the spotlight
I'm out of time

Those lines pose a riddle I'm not sure anyone could answer, except maybe Hunter or Paul Hewson and they are both dead. Is the sunshine another name for the spotlight, or is it the opposite – day to the spotlight's night? We've already been told in the verse that there is no day or night on the stage, just colours. And if the singer is wasting time in the daylight, on the stage he is out of time. Does he mean *outside of* time, as in the vast timelessness of space, where Plato believed the truth resided? Or does he mean rhythmically out of step, a reference to the irregular beat that tries to trip him at the start of every verse line? Or is it that he has perhaps seen his own time running out? That last possibility becomes stronger in the next verse, which is freighted with fatalism.

There's no regrets
My case is closed
Lost man found his road in the end
And the last petal leaves the rose

After this there are no more vocal verses, just two different bridges, and with the first comes an unexpected burst of defiance. Hunter, suddenly revived, sounds as though his fate might not be predetermined after all. *Elevator take me high, take me to the street*, he cries, as the band strike power chords behind him. He's climbing out of the earth, escaping the grave, only the elevator leaves him at street level (which, after all, is where he has asked to be taken), right back where his burdens began. And this is where we find him again in the final bridge, talking to a cigarette-smoking ballerina – like him, a creature of the Broadway night – who can offer no solace, only this statement of resignation to the fleeting and impermanent nature of existence:

Boy, the world is just a stairway
How can I understand
When my world turns to sand?

But this isn't Broadway. Hunter, Hewson, the ballerina, they are all in Goneville.

And what about the boy who left Gonville for a life of rock 'n' roll? By the end of the '50s Johnny Devlin had moved to Australia, where he would sustain, into the next decade, a mid-level career as an antipodean rocker. When The Beatles toured Australasia in 1964 at the height of Beatlemania, Johnny returned to New Zealand as the band's opening act. He had a suit made especially for the occasion: imitation leather, shiny black, with sparking diamante buttons. At The Beatles' first press conference, Paul McCartney was asked a question about what was fashionable in rock 'n' roll nowadays. 'Leather?' said McCartney. 'No. Leather's out.'

15
PREPARATIONS

By the autumn of 1977 I was in Rough Justice and attending my first rehearsals. Unlike Rick's earlier band Mammal, Rough Justice didn't include any songwriters so we were restricted to playing covers. That seemed okay: most professional bands on the circuit did other people's material. Local radios were thumping out the disco beat of KC and The Sunshine Band's 'I'm Your Boogie Man' and Rose Royce's 'Car Wash', or oozing the creamy concoctions of The Eagles' *Hotel California* and Fleetwood Mac's *Rumours*, but we didn't learn anything by these groups. Rick's selections were mostly '60s rhythm and blues standards – B.B. King's 'The Thrill Is Gone', Otis Redding's 'Dock of the Bay', James Brown's 'Papa's Got a Brand New Bag'. I loved to hear him sing songs like these. Playing their basslines made me feel like I was laying the foundation stones of a cathedral. We also learned an Al Green song I suggested, 'Take Me to the River'. A track from one of his albums, it was not well known but had a wonderful bassline and a lyric that seemed to conflate baptism and sex, and Rick sang it with all the gravity I'd expected.

We also mastered a couple of fairly recent songs – Thelma Houston's disco hit 'Don't Leave Me This Way' and Stevie Wonder's 'I Wish' – and a few by The Rolling Stones, hoping these might be enough to satisfy an audience wanting to hear something familiar. But mostly we designed our repertoire to please ourselves.

By now I had met the other musicians Rick had enlisted. Peter Kennedy, our lead guitarist, was the elder brother of Richard Kennedy, the spectacular southpaw from Country Flyers. He was thin, straw-haired, extremely pale, and looked hardly strong enough to lift a guitar, let alone play one. On our first meeting he gave me a tentative handshake and a pleasant smile. Rick had told me confidentially he was taking a gamble hiring him. While Rick was in prison, Peter had begun taking heroin. He had developed a reputation for unreliability and hadn't gigged in two years. Now he was off smack and trying to stay straight. Rick hoped the responsibility of a regular gig would keep him that way.

Peter and Rick were good friends and had known each other since the late '60s, when they had been both flatmates and bandmates. I listened as they reminded each other of the various occasions their flat had been raided by the drug squad. 'Remember,' Peter said. 'You were in your room and called out, "Hide the stash, Peter, I think the cops are coming." But the cops were already in the house. One of them found me upstairs and asked, "Are you Peter? Your mate says to hide the stash. He thinks the cops are coming."' Both hooted at the memory. Rick's head tilted back, his eyes scrunched up, and his throat emitted the long staccato chortle I quickly learnt was an indication something had gone either very right or very wrong.

Rick had also found a piano player called Simon who was about the same age as me, with a silver stud through his nose and shoulder-length blond hair that he frequently flicked back from his eyes. I was dismayed to learn his preference was for arty white English groups such as 10cc and Supertramp: what Rick sang best, and what I wanted to play, were deep R&B songs.

Rick was still looking for a drummer so I suggested Martin Highland, my friend from school. Soon he was part of the band as well, along with another of our Onslow gang, Stephen Jessup. Although Stephen was primarily a guitarist, the idea that he doubled on saxophone and had a bus driver's licence appealed to Rick. And then there was Janet Clouston. We didn't have a manager, sound mixer, lighting designer, wardrobe assistant, roadie, door person or any of the other extra-musical operatives a professional band usually carried in its retinue. Janet's role seemed to include all these things and more.

We started rehearsing in the house next door to Rick's, which happened to be empty. For reasons I never fully grasped, Rick had a key. We would assemble in the house every day, late morning, set up in the unfurnished living room and rehearse until late afternoon.

Rick's cannabis consumption was the stuff of legend. When I was still at school I had heard a whisper that the Mammal singer was a big pot-head, maybe even a dealer. Since then I'd had the opportunity to try pot a few times. Initially I had felt no effect. When friends grinned and grew glassy-eyed after a few puffs, I was convinced they were putting it on. But one night a few of us shared a joint as we walked from downtown up to Kelburn and

I suddenly saw what they had been grinning about. The streets, the city, the whole world had become bright and cartoon-like. We were characters in a comic strip. I noticed a parking meter, mounted on a solid steel bar, lying at the side of the road. It had been put there deliberately for us to find. *Don't follow leaders, watch your parking meters!* We could read each other's minds. Between the three of us we managed to lift it off the ground. It weighed a ton and yet was weightless. We laughed and sang, 'Everybody must get stoned!' as we carried it, without any need for discussion, to the top of vertiginous Everton Terrace where we lived.

Since then I had discovered that sound, like vision, could seem more detailed and absorbing on pot; it could be good for listening to music, especially if I was trying to zone in on the bass parts. But I had never met anyone who smoked like Rick. When he didn't have a joint in his mouth he'd be rolling the next one from a grubby plastic bag of plant matter that he carried down the front of his trousers. The first time he offered me a joint I accepted. 'By the way,' he cautioned, 'this is one-puff stuff.'

I drew deeply and passed it to Martin, who declined and handed it on to Stephen. Rick counted in the song we were working on. It may have been 'Back Stabbers' by The O'Jays, although after a few bars I really had no idea. I had completely lost track of which part of the tune we were playing, the verse or the chorus, or even what the song was. My fingers were strange pink tendrils with minds of their own, moving on the rubbery strings of my bass. It was fascinating to observe them but I didn't know whether I was in control, or whether the notes they were making were even in the same key as the rest of the band's. I had to sit down. As there were no chairs I simply slid to the floor in front of my speaker box and slumped there, inert. No one seemed to notice.

Over the weeks that we rehearsed, the music started to come together. Peter was clearly a superb musician. He drew a bright biting tone from his guitar, a bit like Frank Zappa's sound on *Weasels Ripped My Flesh*, and employed a sense of the surreal. When Rick suggested we needed a two-bar phrase to cue the ending of an Aretha Franklin song, Peter played the opening of Beethoven's Fifth. It fitted perfectly. The rest of us diligently swotted our soul records, trying our best to replicate the originals.

Sometimes neighbours or passers-by would wander in to the house, attracted by the sounds. Usually they would listen for a while, offer some mild encouragement and leave, but one visitor made himself at home. No one knew who he was or how to get rid of him. Rick, who was often uncomfortable in the presence of strangers, seemed particularly agitated. I realised the stranger's presence was inhibiting him from having his customary smoke. The visitor had been there perhaps half an hour, having seated himself in the only chair, lit a cigarette and helped himself to somebody's beer, when I noticed through the window a couple of men in suits walking purposefully up the zigzag path.

'Who are those guys?' I wondered aloud. The song we were practising ground to a halt. Rick, deep inside the melody, kept singing until all the instruments had fallen silent, at which point he opened his eyes, looked momentarily confused, then saw what the rest of us were looking at. The men had reached the front door. 'Fuck. The cops.' He rushed out the back. Some of the band followed.

The knock came. It turned out the men were real-estate agents, assigned to look over the property. One asked what we were doing there. None of us could really say. After a few minutes Rick reappeared, composure regained, and explained we were there with the knowledge and permission of the owners and were keeping an eye on the place to ensure no undesirables took advantage of its apparent abandonment. They seemed to accept his story. Somewhere in the melee the mysterious guest fled. He was never seen again.

One evening after a rehearsal we went to Carmen's Balcony, a strip club run by Wellington's famous drag queen. I had never been to a strip club before and would have been unlikely to visit one on this or any other night if it hadn't been that Midge Marsden's Country Flyers were playing there. We scaled a set of stairs, paid the cover charge and arrived in a dim smoky room with large mirrors on crimson walls. It was as though I'd stepped off Victoria Street into pre-war Berlin.

The crowd was a combination of what I assumed were regulars – middle-aged guys in dirty suits, glamorously seedy types of indeterminate gender, night people – and others I might have seen at rock shows. Like the shared corridor between the bars of the Royal Tiger, it was a weird collision of subcultures, yet no one was made to feel unwelcome. Alcohol was quaffed from paper cups, filled on the sly from bottles in bags under tables. Cigarette smoke choked the air.

Soon the lights went down and a spotlight picked out on the raised stage a figure dressed in grubby white, with greased black hair, a pencil moustache and dark glasses. In a raw Kiwi accent he introduced himself as Neville Purvis 'at your service', master

of ceremonies for Cabaret Capital Strut. He proceeded to give a droll account of his history as a small-time Hutt Valley crim. 'I went to Taita College and Mount Crawford finishing school,' he told us, Mount Crawford being Wellington's infamous prison. After offering smatterings of street wisdom – 'The Mark II Zephyr is the pinnacle of twentieth-century technology, you should see the size of the back seat, and that's Neville on the level' – he introduced a series of sketches. These included political satire (a woman wore a pig mask that bore an obvious resemblance to prime minister Robert Muldoon), musical interludes from the Flyers, poetic rants from Alan Brunton, fire-eating, and even a cameo by Carmen herself, singing the standard 'Autumn Leaves' in a tremulous baritone.

The nearest thing I'd experienced to this was a Blerta show, but there I had been just an onlooker. Here I was being watched by people as curious as I was to see who else belonged to this Wellington demi-monde. Neville Purvis, I later learned, was Arthur Baysting, a poet and songwriter, but the driving force behind the cabaret were Red Mole, a theatre troupe founded by Brunton, Sally Rodwell and Deborah Hunt. The relationship with Carmen had begun when Deborah and Sally, short of income, had approached her and offered to augment her strip shows with topless dancing and fire-eating. This had led to Red Mole being offered a Sunday night slot. Their show had quickly expanded to become the main attraction, ultimately running four nights a week. Each month it was completely revised. One season was themed around New Zealand in the 1950s. Another, on the '60s, was called *Holyoake's Children*. Over the next few months Carmen's Balcony became a regular haunt.

During breaks in Rough Justice rehearsals, if Rick wasn't sharing his knowledge about the history of the Balkans or the novels of George Eliot, or on the phone arranging band bookings and other unspecified business, he would roll another joint and outline his plan for the band. He had given up his job at the university after being busted for pot. The university had been very tolerant, he said, but he hadn't wanted to embarrass them any more. The band would be full-time and professional. He couldn't offer us a wage but promised us an equal share of the earnings after expenses. Professionalism meant, among other things, a dress code. It wasn't strict but he drew the line at sandals and brown corduroy. That left open the opportunities for flared denim, striped sailor shirts, brocaded waistcoats and other fashion crimes too awful to recall.

Where would we be playing? The universities were where the more experimental and original bands could still find an audience. Bruce Kirkland, Graeme Nesbitt's successor at the Student Arts Council, had refined the university touring circuit. Hippie happenings had evolved into well-organised rock tours. An extensive campus tour had been vital in the launching of Split Enz. Now Split Enz were in Britain on the brink of international fame. But we had doubts. Would the students of '77 have any use for our vintage rhythm and blues? And even if they did, the occasional university hop or campus tour could not support six full-time musicians.

There were two ways most working musicians could make a living. One was to secure a residency in a nightclub or restaurant. That door was closed to Rough Justice. Our repertoire was too esoteric for the nightclubs, which favoured covers of the Top 20, and we were certainly no dine-and-dance act.

The other way was to tour the pubs. This often meant dealing with grouchy publicans with permanent hangovers, who saw musicians as a necessary evil and told them so. However, a few venues were more welcoming. One was The Cabana in Napier. Frequented by sailors and ship-girls, it was managed by Charlie, a bottle-blonde matriarch who would greet musicians with a glass of wine in one hand and a cigarette in the other, feed them three-course meals, and be always the last to leave the house bar after the post-gig party.

The Cabana was independently owned, but most pubs belonged to one of the two giant breweries, Dominion and Lion. One evening Rough Justice made a reconnaissance visit to the Lion Tavern on Wellington's Molesworth Street, where we hoped we would soon get a gig. If the Royal Tiger was an outpost of Lion Breweries' operations, this was their central headquarters. It had been designed by the company's architecture department in a style known as 'brutalist', a word coined in the '50s by British architects Alison and Peter Smithson, who adapted it from 'beton brut', a phrase used by Le Corbusier: beton for concrete, brut for rough or unrefined.

I'm beginning to see that 'brut' represents more than just the rawness of the two-storey fortress as I contemplate the grim bald bouncer guarding the door at the top of the first tier of concrete steps. I am still a year shy of the legal age to enter pubs, but the bouncer is more concerned about Stephen's flared denim trousers.

'No jeans,' he states firmly.

'But the sign says no *black* jeans,' Stephen reasons. 'These are dark blue, and anyway they are dress jeans.'

The bouncer grunts, but he is already conducting a wardrobe inspection of the next customers in the queue so we hurry up the remaining steps to the Spectrum Bar. Inside, the light is low, the air a smoky fug, the carpet sticky with beer. Raised voices battle the sound of a five-piece band, Fragments of Time, which is playing in front of a painted backdrop of swirling oranges and browns. Originally called Father Time, the band have recently renamed themselves after a membership reshuffle, and in a few weeks will rebrand themselves yet again as Mi-Sex. In this final guise they will find Australasian fame, with a string of hit singles and albums. Tonight, though, they are still a pub band, one of many currently making their living on the Lion Breweries' circuit.

Their set consists mainly of covers. Their animated performance makes up for the static lighting. Their singer Steve Gilpin, a winner of television's *New Faces* competition, wears dark glasses and has the confident stance of a stadium rock star, although he is playing to only 150 people. Bass player Don Martin does balletic things with his hands, while guitarist Kevin Stanton performs full-body gymnastics. At one point Stanton does a cartwheel on the cramped stage, navigating with an apparent sixth sense the jungle of obstacles – pointed microphone stands, uncoiled cables, sharp-edged cymbals and glowing amplifiers.

'You should have seen him last night,' I overhear one of the band's crew say. 'He was doing that, off his head on acid.'

Rough Justice might not be able to compete with that kind of showmanship, but is there a place for well-intentioned tributes to our R&B heroes on the pub circuit? That decision is in one man's hands.

16
'NOT THE MUSICAL GENIUS BUSINESS'

People who encountered Richard Holden always remarked on his hands. 'The size of mutton hams,' was how one journalist described them. Another compared them to dinner plates, and yet another to 'twin kilos of corned silverside'. And it was not just his hands. Holden was, said impresario Alan Smythe, 'larger than life, with a frame and countenance to match' and 'one of life's great gargantuan, Rabelaisian characters'.

Unlike Rabelais, the Renaissance monk and scholar who wrote the bawdy, extravagant novels *Gargantua and Pantagruel*, Holden was of humble origin. Born in 1948, he was two years old when his parents separated. After this he and his twin brother Alistair lived with their mother, first in Trentham, then in a state house in Naenae. When they were eleven their mother packed them off to Motuihe Island in the Hauraki Gulf, where their father ran a navy canteen. They hadn't been there long when they received a telegram: 'Don't come back, it's your father's turn now.'

Schools and books held little interest for the young Richard. By fifteen he had left school, unqualified, and was dressing

windows for Wiseman's electrical goods store in Auckland's Queen Street. On the weekends he would help a friend who was converting an old picture theatre in Milford into a ballroom. Once the Surfside Ballroom opened, he was kept busy at the weekend dances, blowing up balloons and operating the spotlight.

In 1970 he brought his puff and panache to Wellington, taking a job as Lion Breweries' display and merchandising manager. Based in the corporation's offices in Molesworth Street, he dressed windows of taverns and dance floors of lounge bars. When Quinn's Post Hotel in Upper Hutt ran a nine-week talent quest, he had the stage painted magenta and the house piano purple. By the time the Lion Tavern opened the following year, with its live music venue the Spectrum Bar, Richard Holden had been promoted to national entertainment manager.

The first band he contracted was Triangle, centred on the piano playing and bravura singing of Dennis O'Brien. Then came Tapestry, a slick covers band fronted by brothers Dave and Wayne Feehan, whose high quavering voices provided a simulacrum of The Bee Gees. These groups were soon succeeded by The Quincy Conserve, a tight septet led by a short tough taskmaster with an intense reedy voice, who had played professionally since his early teens, toured the Pacific with showbands, studied arrangement at the New South Wales Conservatorium of Music, and went by the name of Malcolm Hayman. He had been lured back to New Zealand in 1967 by his mother, who had claimed to be on her deathbed, and formed the Quincys in time to cash in on the craze for jazz-tinged brassy rock bands such as Chicago and Blood, Sweat & Tears.

The Quincys were extremely professional, quick to master new material, and some of them had sight-reading chops. They could back anyone, from teen pop performer Mr Lee Grant to jazz virtuoso Ricky May. They appeared on TV pop shows and children's programmes, and were the house band at Wellington's HMV studios, providing backup on records by middle-of-the-road singers such as Craig Scott and Suzanne, as well as making records under their own name. Hayman didn't write songs but he was canny in his choice of covers. 'Alright in the City' and 'Aire of Good Feeling', originally by Sonny Charles and The Ides of March respectively, were unknown compositions from overseas that the Quincys successfully turned into national hits.

Their best record, though, was a rare Quincys' original. In 1969 Bruno Lawrence had returned to Wellington from a stint in Australia. Urgently needing a gig to support his wife and young children, he had finagled his way into the band. Lawrence's free spirit and Hayman's staunch disciplinarianism were never going to be a good fit, and it all came spectacularly undone in front of a watching nation during a live telecast of the Loxene Golden Disc Awards. A drunk and manic Bruno, on crutches after an accident, upstaged Hayman with an arresting mime routine. Mocking the fact the band were playing to a pre-recorded track, he waved his sticks wildly through the air, rarely making contact with his drums. He later invited the director general of the New Zealand Broadcasting Corporation to 'kiss my crutch'. But this was not before he had written Hayman the brilliant 'Ride the Rain', a national hit that maximised the Quincys' strengths with brassy fanfares, jazzy breakdowns, a ferocious wah-wah guitar solo and a subtly trippy lyric.

The Quincys had held a longstanding residency at Wellington's Downtown Club. Managed by Roy and Joy Young, who also ran a late-night café, Casablanca, the club was open from eight 'til late, Thursday to Sunday, and was packed on weekends. Situated by the waterfront, it was a magnet to visiting sailors. It was not licensed – liquor licences being almost impossible for nightclubs to obtain – so alcohol was smuggled in and discreetly added to cups of Coke. The Quincys played up to five sets a night, and were paid a weekly salary of $55 each.

Late in 1972 Richard Holden lured the group away with a promise of better pay, shorter hours, smarter dressing rooms and legal booze. The Downtown Club never recovered from the loss of the Quincys and the arrival of legislation allowing pubs to stay open until ten o'clock. By the end of the year it had been rechristened the Downtown Disco Club and had replaced live music with a disc jockey. 'Jet Set Top D.J. Paul Mack Plus! Plus! Plus! PULSATING LIGHTING EFFECTS' screamed the *Evening Post* listing. Such novelties failed to reverse the venue's fortunes and it closed, to be reborn in 1973 as Ziggy's and run by a cooperative cashing in, with some success, on the glam rock fad.

At the Spectrum Bar, the Quincys played their own sets of brassy covers, and most weeks backed a visiting star. *New Faces* supplied a lot of the guests. Singers Dean Waretini and Steve Gilpin were frequently backed by the Quincys, as were other TV celebrities such as Ray Woolf and Rob Guest. At a time when New Zealand had only one television channel, all viewers saw the same thing so these artists were familiar and drew big crowds.

New and refurbished taverns were opening up all over the country, with music the magnet they hoped would lure the drinkers. Holden explained to the *New Zealand Herald*: 'People do not want just to sit and drink a jug of beer. They want to be entertained. If they are not being entertained they stay away.'

Richard Holden had firm ideas about how musicians should conduct themselves, both on stage and off. I recently learned about the Holden rulebook from a woman called Jackie Matthews, whose acquaintance I made through a Facebook group concerned with the history of Wellington's nightlife. Back then Jackie was engaged to Malcolm Hayman, and she remembers Holden yelling at musicians to behave themselves, be on time and do the job properly.

Holden sent Hayman and Matthews on a tour of the taverns to set up and fine-tune the sound systems. 'It was like a huge honeymoon,' Matthews told me. 'He paid for our accommodation, all our travel, everything. I came back pregnant so I said, "Okay Richard, you were the cause of this so I'm going to name my baby Richard."'

With the bars set up for entertainment, Holden's next task was to find bands. There were hundreds of local outfits on offer but few met his criteria. 'We have to get away from the idea of four guys getting together and forming a group just because they like each other, and instead get guys who are getting together to do a job,' he told the *Herald*. 'Musicians have to realise they are a product that can be sold.'

Auckland-based Tommy Ferguson's Goodtime Band filled the brief ('features a girl saxophone player,' honked the press release) and were offered a two-year contract. But work on the circuit eluded a university band such as Mammal, who did not style themselves as a product. Holden evidently did not regard them as something he could sell. When music journalist John Dix, briefly employed to assist with promotion at the Lion Tavern, suggested Holden try out the campus stars, Holden scoffed, 'You can't book Mammal. Their audience drinks orange juice and we need to sell beer.'

It is unlikely Holden would have liked Mammal's repertoire any more than he approved of their audience's drinking habits. To *Herald* columnist John Berry he said: 'There has been a tendency for musicians to play for themselves instead of the customers. There has been some good original music but a lot of original rubbish. They will have to realise that we're not in the musical genius business. We're in the entertainment business.'

The Quincys were the rare band who met Holden's stringent standards, but the number of Lion venues around the country was growing rapidly and the Quincys couldn't be in all of them at once. Sometimes they would go out of town for a weekend and play at one or other of the refurbished taverns, but they were usually occupied in Molesworth Street, backing entertainers and playing their own sets.

Holden found part of the solution offshore. Since the Second World War and the American occupation, the Philippines had been famous for producing well-drilled bands that could provide flawless facsimiles of popular records. Soon Holden was arranging work visas for Filipino performers such as The Constellations and Royal Flush, tuxedoed show bands who would spend six months or more touring the Lion circuit.

From Los Angeles came a band purporting to be The Ink Spots. In 1967 a US federal judge had ruled that as so many groups had purloined the name it had become public domain and was free for anyone to use. At the time there were up to a hundred different Ink Spots line-ups touring the world. Holden's Ink Spots were led by a man named George Holmes and included no original members.

Holden would also go to London to audition prospective acts, inviting them to take tea with him at the Dorchester. He later boasted that 'some were so cowed by the snootiness of the place they lowered their asking price'.

Holden's ultimate answer to controlling the style of entertainment was to form bands himself. His first creation was The Distillery.

He handpicked the line-up, dictated the musical style, chose the outfits, and gave the band a name that left little doubt who the master was. One of the musicians was a drummer I had first seen at the Union Hall. Paul Davies had played there with Tamburlaine, although he had got his start at school dances and church halls as a schoolboy in Rotorua.

In 2014, sitting in his apartment overlooking a leafy corner of the Auckland University campus, Davies told me about arriving in Wellington. He had enrolled at Victoria University. Stepping off the Cable Car in Kelburn, the provincial teenager saw the cathedral-like Hunter Building and felt as though he was at Oxford. Late for his first lecture, Philosophy 101, he nervously took the nearest place at a table where three other students were sitting. At the end of the class they introduced themselves: Rick Bryant, Bill Lake and Tony Backhouse. Before long Davies had joined Rick in one of the ever-changing line-ups of Rick and The Rockets. He went on to play with Tamburlaine as they evolved from their acoustic folk roots into a more traditional rock band, then with a dine-and-dance quartet who held a residency at The Woolshed, one of a growing number of licensed restaurants offering entertainment. It had long been his ambition to be able to write 'musician' on his tax return.

After a year at The Woolshed he got the call from Holden. 'He rang me at home and asked if I could join. "Then get your drums," he said, "put them in the car and come to Hamilton now. You'll have to play tonight."'

That night The Distillery were backing Eddie Calvert, that strange reactionary English trumpet player. Also handpicked by Holden was Steve McDonald, a flamboyant career musician who had been the drummer in a band called Timberjack, which had enjoyed a national hit in 1970 with a curious satanic novelty, 'Come to the Sabbat'. McDonald sat behind an impressive array of keyboards. The singer-guitarist was Peter Caulton, who had held a long residency at the Royal Oak Tavern and founded the Country Flyers before leaving them in the hands of Midge Marsden.

Davies remembers Caulton as 'a kind of Titahi Bay surf club good-time boy. Told a few jokes, looked like a football player. A hard-case party boy.' Steve McDonald boasted one of the first mellotrons in New Zealand. 'You pressed a key and it had a bank of tapes. You could summon up the Vienna Boys' Choir,' Davies recalled. 'It was a heavy thing. Three or four of us used to lug it around between gigs.

'Richard made us wear dinner suits and dress like gangsters – homburgs, black and white shoes. There was a poster with a couple of us holding plastic machine guns, sitting on the bonnet of an old Packard with a couple of models. That was the image.'

One day Holden summoned the band to the Lion office in downtown Auckland. They were to wear full regalia: double-breasted satin lapels, bow ties and white platform shoes. He ordered them to walk down Queen Street, where he had arranged for a photographer from the *Herald* to snap them. 'It was anathema to me but he did things like that,' Davies said. 'It was promotion. But we were on a pretty good salary. Employer: Lion Breweries. Vocation: musician.'

Eddie Calvert was just the first of many entertainers Davies would back during his Distillery stint. Others included Noel McKay, a 'sixty-year-old female impersonator accompanied by

his eighty-year-old wife Tess, and a guy called Terry who ran with the epithet Australia's Mr Rock 'n' Roll, sort of a Jerry Lee Lewis piano-playing soundalike'.

But there were musical rewards, such as working with Ricky May. This virtuoso vocalist had played nightclubs around New

Zealand – including a residency at Wellington's Sorrento, with Bruno Lawrence on drums – before moving to Australia in 1962 when he was just nineteen. Holden brought May home in 1974 for a tour of the Lion circuit. 'We had three hired Hillman Avengers,' Davies remembers, 'and Ricky always came with me. Somehow he'd got the impression that whatever town we were in I'd know somebody he could buy pot from.

'We both loved jazz and we both liked Sinatra. I sort of grew up on jazz – my mother was a fan – so Ricky and I connected quite well. We'd play an opening piece, then anything could happen, anything at all. One night at the Lion Tavern while he was singing he came up and said into my ear, "Don't you fucking know 'Roll Over Beethoven'?" I said, "Of course I do." "Well sing it!" He took over the drums and there I was, out front in a dinner suit and sandshoes. He was a bugger like that. But a brilliant musician.'

The Distillery was not the last alcohol-themed band on the Breweries' roster. Over the next two years the circuit would see names such as Auckland group Beam (as in Jim Beam bourbon) and Pilsener, a six-piece combo from the Rhondda Valley in South Wales, renamed by Holden to promote Lion's latest lager.

By the mid '70s Richard Holden was managing an entertainment budget upwards of two million a year, roughly $22 million in today's money. 'As well as providing our younger patrons with the best musical entertainment there is available, we are assisting to foster professional music in this country,' Lion's general manager, John Macfarlane, announced in *Brewnews*, the company's bimonthly publication. 'For the first time we are offering a secure and continuing opportunity for professional groups, who no longer have to concern themselves with trying to fit in part-time outside employment with their musical commitments.'

Holden's approach didn't always win him friends, particularly among the other booking agents. Mike Corless had started out in the late '60s as a drummer in Hawke's Bay before founding a series of agencies that would keep him in the music business for more than four decades. These days he is wiry, greying and goateed, with a twinkle in his eye and rock 'n' roll teeth.

'I can't remember anything, Nick,' he says. 'I'm hopeless. But come on, you can jog my memory.' We are sitting in St Kevins Arcade on Auckland's Karangahape Road waiting for coffee. 'Well,' I say, 'how did you get started in the management business?'

'It started with ten o'clock closing,' he says. 'People like Bobby Davis, Ray Woolf, Bunny Walters, all the television stars who used to work the cabarets started working the pubs. I started Topline Entertainment in Hastings. We were booking them to come and play with a local band. They would have to rehearse first of all, then work the pubs for two or three nights. There were a lot of bands in Hastings, a lot of Māori bands that were really good.'

Provincial resistance to cover charges eventually drove Corless to Auckland, where he and Bobby Davis started Davco Promotions. Their biggest act was Maori Volcanics, a six-piece show band who had spent most of the '60s touring internationally, from Vegas to Vietnam. The band had a flawless stage show that incorporated standards, soul tunes and comedy, and was the launch pad for the career of the great comedian Billy T. James. Corless sought venues for the Volcanics that were outside the Lion circuit, sometimes having to build stage and sound systems from scratch.

Holden competed aggressively. 'First we were up against these Filipino show bands,' Corless remembers. 'They were really good – slick and tight and together. But when the Volcanics came in he tried to take over the whole scene, going to Australia and bringing back bands like The Maori Hi-Five.'

The much-loved Volcanics drew good crowds to the biggest non-Lion venues Corless could find: Pakuranga's White Horse Inn, North Shore's Thunderbird Valley Inn, Hastings' Mayfair Hotel, and Broderick Inn in Johnsonville, where they recorded a live album in 1975. But Holden held the trump card. Most of the pubs big enough to host bands of the Volcanics' stature were Lion-owned. He banned Davco's acts from them.

ROCK N ROLL

17
ON THE BUS

On a bright blue day the Rough Justice bus lumbered off the ferry and lurched south, down the Kaikoura coast, mountains towering to the right, waves breaking to the left. For the two months we'd been rehearsing, our touring vehicle had remained stationary on the slope outside Rick's house, along with his various dead cars. I hadn't been even sure it had an engine. Now, loaded with musical equipment and personal luggage, it was rumbling along at a steady 40 kilometres an hour, taking us on our first outing, a five-week tour of the South Island.

In practical terms a bus is a good way of getting six or seven musicians, their gear, crew and hangers-on from one gig to the next. It can double as a dressing room when the venue doesn't have one, or a bunkroom when accommodation is scarce. But a bus means more than that. The prototype was the bus that Ken Kesey, the American novelist turned acid-evangelist, bought in 1964 after selling the film rights to *One Flew Over the Cuckoo's Nest*. He had it decorated with psychedelic designs, filled it with the friends and followers he called his Merry Pranksters, plus a supply of LSD, which was still legal at the time, and set out from California. The destination sign read FURTHUR, although the journey was actually a round trip via New York, which Tom Wolfe would chronicle in his 1968 book *The Electric Kool-Aid Acid Test*.

Following Kesey's example, house trucks and technicolour motorhomes started popping up all over the world, including in New Zealand. Blerta and Mammal had buses. A bus made a statement. The bands who played local residencies then packed their gear into Hillman Avengers and drove back to their homes in the suburbs were just day trippers, weekend rock 'n' rollers. A bus signified a commitment not just to making music but to the whole philosophy of freedom and defiance that went with it.

The southern stretch of State Highway One is quiet. We have been driving for miles without seeing another vehicle. Rick is at the wheel, muttering something partway between the commentary of a tour bus driver and an internal monologue. 'You can get fucking good crayfish just up here at the right time of year. In fact it might be worth stopping,' he says, as we pass through the little settlement of Rakautara. Janet is sitting up front beside him. The rest of us are sprawled at the back on mattresses covering our equipment. Someone with a battery-operated cassette player puts on a Miles Davis album but the sound from the small speakers is drowned out by the bellowing of the engine. It doesn't feel as though I'm on my way to work, but rather setting out on a holiday with an unusual but congenial new family.

Our first gig is at a tavern operated by Dominion Breweries in Timaru. Lion also has a tavern here; we read in the *Timaru Herald* that Pilsener, Holden's Welsh band, are playing there that night. The tavern management puts us up in an old single-storey brick house. Evidence of the bands that have stayed here before us can be found in felt marker on the bathroom walls. One group, Skylord, have shown extra class by having their logo designed and printed on a sticker. One of these is stuck to the inside of the toilet bowl. There are cigarette burns on the tables and windowsills, and a single-bar heater in the living room, which we cluster around to write the evening's set list. We each have our own bedroom, which I will soon discover is not something you can always count on.

That night, for the first time, we try out our set on a paying audience. It's a small crowd: it seems most Timaruvians have gone to see Pilsener. We race nervously from song to song, as though pausing for more than a beat may force us to engage in closer communication with our audience. I look at Rick. He has sweat running down his forehead, his neck and the back of his shirt, and his eyes are scrunched shut. Peter is playing lovely lyrical lines on his guitar, although at one point he turns around, kicks his amplifier and yells at it unintelligibly, a ritual I will see enacted many times over the next two and a half years.

Returning to the house at the end of the night, another ritual is initiated: the post-gig post-mortem. Who counted that song in at the wrong tempo? Weren't the stops in this song supposed to be in the third verse, not the second? Which was the song that got them up dancing and what made them sit down again?

The second night goes a little better. Our nerves have settled and the crowd has grown. The tiled dance area, marked out in flashing fairy lights, fills during the final set. Christchurch, a few nights later, is better still. There are people in the crowd who remember Rick from Mammal days and have come especially to hear him sing. Someone compliments us on our tricky arrangement of 'I Heard It through the Grapevine', which we've modelled on the Gladys Knight version, rather than the better-known one by Marvin Gaye.

We move on to Ashburton, Dunedin, Invercargill. Sometimes in the bus I sit up front beside Rick and take in one of his endlessly digressive lectures. He starts telling me about the soul singer Joe Tex. This leads into an analysis of Tolstoy and winds up with the history of the New Zealand labour movement. It feels as though

I have stayed at university, although it's hard to say what paper I have enrolled in.

Rick also instructs me about drugs. His attitude to pot is self-evident and I'm starting to suspect his use of the drug partly accounts for his free-associative tutorial style, but he is by no means an advocate of wholesale drug use. He was wary of LSD for a long time, he tells me, and still advises taking it only under the most 'copacetic' conditions. The things he can remember doing on Mandrax are apparently too embarrassing to share. He pauses, then emits one of his customary chortles. He turns serious at the subject of heroin. It is lethal and destructive, he says. Anyone who sells it is evil, anyone who takes it is committing suicide, and in his band it is strictly forbidden.

Rick may smoke as much pot as all of Bob Marley's Wailers put together, but although he generously offers it to us no one else has anything like his capacity or enthusiasm for it. The truth is, we members of Rough Justice are not the decadent stereotypes our appearance might suggest. On days off between gigs we go sightseeing in the bus. This carries its own risks. One day, crossing Christchurch's Port Hills and negotiating the narrow coastal road to Akaroa, we encounter torrential rain. Bets are taken on which misfortune will claim the bus first: falling rocks or washed-out roads. Or perhaps Stephen, who is driving, will fail to navigate one of the endless bends and plunge us all into the bay? Somehow we make it back alive.

In Dunedin we take a winding road to the clifftops above St Clair with the engine belching fumes and overheating. At the steepest part the steaming vehicle refuses to go any further so we get out and walk the final distance to the ruins of Cargill's Castle.

Here, stepping on to a non-existent floor, I grab a wooden beam just in time to stop falling several metres into a concrete pit.

Outside in the long grass, Stephen is practising handstands, something I have known him to do ever since we were at school. We would be walking along a street and I'd suddenly realise I was talking to a pair of shoes while Stephen's head was bobbing upside down, a few inches above the pavement. This time, he has done a vertical flip and is moving backwards, grinning at us. Janet is the first to see that the gentle meadow ends abruptly at the edge of a cliff, which is now just behind him. She lunges and grabs him as he's about to plummet 150 metres into the Pacific Ocean.

We are safer exploring the provincial junk shops, where Janet finds clothes and naïve art and Rick buys books, musical instruments and crockery decorated with crustaceans. He advises me on second-hand record buys. 'That's a fucking great album you won't see very often,' he confirms as I invest my last seven dollars in a double LP of Howlin' Wolf. Martin has brought a portable record player. We set it up in our motel, and the profound groove and plantation holler of 'Moaning in the Moonlight' rings through the corridors until someone, deaf to genius, threatens to call the manager.

Back in Wellington, our first hometown gig is also our introduction to Hello Sailor, for whom we open at a Victoria University dance. They have come from Auckland and are playing in the capital for the first time. Formed in 1974 on the top floor of Dragon's Ponsonby flat, 'Mandrax Mansion', Hello Sailor has a frontline of former jug band musician Graham Brazier, sometime Beam guitarist Harry Lyon and his old schoolmate Dave McArtney. They aren't prog: they have neither the chops nor the inclination for that. Instead they draw on the fundamentals of twin-guitar rock 'n' roll – Rolling Stones, Velvet Underground – while adding some of the louche artiness of Roxy Music and David Bowie. By this time they have refined their cool to an icy perfection. Close in age, and with connections reaching back to childhood, they have that sense of common identity and purpose characteristic of great bands. Like The Beatles or Stones, they obviously belong together.

As for Rough Justice, our set has gained some polish over the five weeks in the South Island, but performing in our hometown for the first time has given us a renewed case of nerves. Rick sings with his usual authority but there is something about our accompaniment that seems the opposite of the spontaneous joy I have heard in great rock and soul records. We seem studied and formal. Perhaps it is because, other than Rick and Peter, we are a band of beginners, students in the school of rock whom Rick has generously taken under his tutelage. But if Rick is our tutor, I am beginning to see that he too regards the music as a study course: at the end of each gig he gives his performance a mark out of ten. Hello Sailor are, in contrast, the bad boys at the back of the room – leering, smirking, ignoring the lesson, then effortlessly getting the top mark. Afterwards someone tells me that Brazier and McArtney have been asking where they can get some heroin.

Over the next year we will run into Sailor at venues around the country. Once we arrive for a weekend at Bell Block Tavern in New Plymouth as they are loading out. They are coming to the end of a tour promoted by a rum importer, and look roadsick. Graham Brazier staggers over to our bus carrying a crate of the sponsor's product. 'Take it, please,' he groans theatrically. 'It's already turned us all into alcoholics.'

18
ENCOUNTERS

Th' Dudes were younger, with even more swagger than Hello Sailor. Rough Justice became aware of them on our first trip to Auckland. We had pulled into Ponsonby around midnight, tired and slightly stupefied by a combination of pot and engine fumes. But before we could head to our accommodation – a flat rented by some other Wellington musicians who had offered us a few mattresses on the floor – we had a job to do.

Putting up posters is a task most bands place in the hands of paid professionals, but our limited budget meant that, as with most things, we had to do it ourselves. A sticky starch paste of flour and water was mixed in buckets and we took to the streets in pairs, pasting up the posters Peter Kennedy had designed (an astronaut playing a saxophone on the moon) anywhere bands had already left their mark. It was sometime after two a.m. when we finally crawled into our sleeping bags on the floor of the Ponsonby crash pad.

At dawn I awoke to a heavy knocking, then a crash. Cops? A booming voice: 'WHO COVERED UP MY POSTERS?'

ROUGH
JUSTICE
PJK
WED TO SAT.
17 --- 27 MAY
CRICKETER'S

I looked up through sleep-fogged eyes to catch a glimpse of silver hair and a florid face.

'Who the fuck are you?' someone only slightly more sentient mumbled from the other side of the room.

'I'm Charley Gray. I manage Th' Dudes, and you lot have covered up my posters. You have even stuck one of your posters on the side of our van. What are you going to do about that?'

Rick appeared, fully awake after having slept in the bus. 'I'm sorry, there's obviously been a mistake,' he began in his most reassuring tones. 'But look, there's something I've been meaning to talk to you about.' He steered Charley towards the door and I didn't hear any more. Rick's diplomatic skills must have been at their best though: he returned to let us know he had secured a booking at Charley's Island of Real Café in central Auckland's Airedale Street.

When, still wary from our encounter with the proprietor, we arrived at Island of Real a few weeks later for our soundcheck it was to find the curtain to the tiny backstage area decorated with a silver cardboard star bearing the name 'RICK'. On the dressing table inside, an ashtray sported several large ready-rolled joints.

The Island of Real would become one of our favourite out-of-town gigs. Independent and alcohol-free, its name suggested an oasis of integrity, in contrast to the breweries' money-driven enterprises. Charley's wife Anne and the couple's children were always around and there was a welcoming, homely atmosphere. Although Charley continued to have a brusque manner he seemed to like our music. He had been a jazz drummer and in the breaks would play selections from his own record collection. This was where I first heard the sly and swinging 1940s' recordings of

Louis Jordan, which revealed to me where the music of Chuck Berry and B.B. King had originated.

One night we cancelled a Thursday night booking at the Island of Real when we realised everyone else in Auckland would be at a Bob Dylan concert. The news that Dylan was to play in New Zealand for the first time was like being told that tickets were available for the Second Coming. Hiding from public view for much of the past decade had made Dylan more myth than man. The thought of his setting foot in Auckland was surreal.

Reality was bent further out of shape the day before the concert. I was walking out of a bar in Vulcan Lane, where I had arranged to have an afternoon beer with a friend who hadn't showed up, when I saw Dylan strolling past, an arm's length away. I set off in the same direction.

At the intersection of Vulcan Lane and High Street we both stopped. Ten thousand song lyrics rushing through my head, I blurted out the only thing I could think of: 'I'm looking forward to your concert tomorrow.' Tilting his head slightly towards me, Dylan nodded. 'Okay, I'll see you there.' He crossed the street and headed up the hill towards the Intercontinental Hotel. I watched him buy a newspaper and disappear into the building. That evening I picked up a copy of the paper. On the front page was a photo of Dylan and the headline: 'Have you seen this man?'

In spite of my human-scale encounter, Dylan seemed no less mythological the next night on the Western Springs stage. With a huge band – backup singers, horns, violins and an army of guitarists – he was a ringmaster in dazzling white jacket and top hat. It was a long show, a parade of hits in busy big-band arrangements. He gave a shout-out to the Highway 61 Motorcycle Club, who were presumably somewhere in the vast crowd.

This tour would be later dismissed by international critics as Dylan's 'Vegas show' and was ill-served by *Bob Dylan at Budokan*, the album recorded live in Japan two weeks before the circus reached New Zealand. But the concert under the stars at Western Springs was the best thing I had ever heard or seen.

A few months later in Auckland we completed a post-gig pack-out in record time and headed to the North Shore to see James Brown. Brown's visit to New Zealand was as unexpected as Dylan's. Despite a career that had spanned almost a quarter of a century and transformed African American music, Brown had had very little exposure on the New Zealand airwaves. Rick revered him as a singer and bandleader and I had pored over the few recordings I could find, trying to untangle the intricate syncopations. Brown's records were like artefacts from a distant civilisation. The idea that he was still a working musician and that New Zealand might feature on his itinerary had never really occurred to me. Fortunately an entrepreneur, Phil Warren, was not just a canny promoter but also a fan. He must have realised there were enough other James Brown fans to make it worth bringing him over.

The venue was Shoreline Cabaret, one of Warren's nightclubs. The regular ticket included supper but our gig meant we wouldn't make it in time for the meal, which we couldn't have afforded anyway. Rick had somehow managed to get us seats just for the concert. I recognised a number of musicians and a few hard-core soul fans, but mostly the crowd seemed to consist of well-dressed couples, there for the supper as much as the show.

I remember the mesmeric groove of Brown's guitarists, seemingly ego-less in their ability to repeat the same lick over and over until James gave them the signal to change, and the hyperactive MC chanting 'James Brown James Brown James Brown James Brown' like a mantra, before the star's entrance and long after his departure. And I remember Brown bringing the entire band to a halt with a traffic cop's hand gesture so he could spend an eternal five minutes putting his bass player through a humiliating set of paces until the sound of the instrument was adjusted to his satisfaction, then smiling at the audience, letting them know it was all a stunt, and saying with a smile, 'I wouldn't want to blow y'all out of here.'

Afterwards we gave a drunk couple a ride back to town. I'm not sure how they came to be on board. Perhaps they had mistaken our bus for the Milford Express. The woman couldn't remember whom she'd just seen but she'd loved his dancing. Her boyfriend said, 'Sure, it wasn't a bad show, but why didn't he do "Fire"?' After a puzzled moment I realised he had confused James Brown with Arthur Brown, an English one-hit-wonder from the '60s, famous for setting fire to his hat.

Our band had spent the past year doing its best to purvey the essence of soul but what I witnessed that night seemed as far from a Rough Justice show as James Brown's hometown, Atlanta, Georgia, was from New Zealand. There were a lifetime's lessons to go home and think about in that single set. I was glad Rick had resisted making an example of his bass player like that.

19
PIG'S HEAD AND PIPI BOLOGNESE

By the end of our first year on the road Rough Justice had a new piano player. Simon had tolerated the rhythm and blues tunes, even performed them with some skill, but he had never hidden his real desire to get hold of a synthesiser and play in a pop group. 'I'm a white boy,' he said, with a shrug. It seemed a fair explanation.

His replacement, Mike Gubb, was a white boy too, but at the keyboard he became a conduit for Ray Charles. He'd rock from side to side, close his eyes and wince in ecstasy as clusters of blue notes fell from his fingertips. Our soul tunes suddenly sounded a whole lot more convincing. We had also been joined by Boyd, the sax player from my old school band. Money was tight but Rick calculated that adding a full-time saxophonist ought to boost our earning power, even as it increased overheads.

Rick's accounting procedures were a mystery to all of us, except possibly Janet. One day, travelling between gigs, he begins to explain them to me. His jean jacket is his office, he says, as he steers the bus with one hand and rolls a joint with the other. One pocket is for receipts, one for accounts receivable, one for his pot, another for … As he pats the breast pocket that is supposed to contain our earnings from the tour so far, a look of horror crosses his face. The pocket is empty. He makes an abrupt U-turn and soon we are back at the motel where we stayed the previous night. Rushing towards our unit we encounter the cleaner, who is just leaving. She hasn't by any chance come across an envelope in one of the rooms, has she? Maybe, but it's all gone into the bin over there, she says, pointing across the courtyard to a large steel dumpster. Somebody tumbles in and remarkably, beneath several metres of cigarette butts, bottles and other motel room detritus, the envelope is found, the cash still warm inside. The band will eat tonight.

Eating is not something we take for granted. There was the time we arrived in Kuaotunu in Coromandel, down to our last two dollars. It was summer, and our entourage included several girlfriends and extended family members along for the ride. The question of how to feed fifteen people on two dollars was solved by Janet and a couple of the hangers-on. At low tide they went down to the estuary and collected tuatua and pipi, which they brought back, boiled, prised from their shells and served with as much spaghetti as a couple of bucks could buy. Someone found milk and flour, and created a white sauce. The Pipi Bolognese, as it was named, might have been improved if it hadn't included so much sand.

In Queenstown we lucked into a gig at an upmarket hotel. At most provincial taverns, if a band were fed at all they were required to eat the complimentary meal – a statutory ham steak and slice of pineapple – in a cramped corner of the staff kitchen, out of sight of paying customers. This time we were served in the dining room and offered the pick of the menu. There were salads. There was even dessert. But the meal was strictly for band members: while we munched, our entourage, including Janet, her sister Alison, and Boyd's partner Bernadine, was left to starve in luxury. Boyd began to sneak paper bags of food out to them until Rick noticed and took him aside. 'I wouldn't risk that if I were you, Boyd,' he warned in a stern whisper. 'It could be very bad for all of us. You realise we're being watched, don't you?'

I wasn't sure whether there was really any surveillance, or what the repercussions might have been had we been caught feeding friends and family, but this mix of paranoia and pessimism often overtook Rick in situations where he was forced to deal with institutional authority. Eventually Janet and Alison took to the streets with drawings they had done of the local landscape, selling them for enough money to supplement the scraps.

In Christchurch that winter, the breast pocket of Rick's jean jacket was empty once again. Boyd was dispatched, clutching our last five dollars, with instructions to buy something to feed the whole band. He returned with a pig's head and placed it on the table, where it sat, hairy, snouty and staring. Repulsed by the sight, I resolved to go hungry and retired to my room, although once the pig's head was cooking in the oven with some rosemary picked from the roadside, I was lured back by the rich warm smell.

Between tours I would return to the comforting chaos of North Terrace. During one of these stays I started going out with Tina, the best friend of my sister Thomasin and our flatmate Sally.

'Going out' is perhaps a misnomer: we seldom went anywhere. The concept of coupledom made Tina uncomfortable, but she spent the occasional night at North Terrace, or I would stay with her in the attic bedroom of her parents' house. Tina, who had long blonde hair and contact lenses, was beautiful and clever, and happiest when making things – puppets or jewellery – or laughing with Thomasin and Sally over numerous cups of tea around the kitchen table. I sometimes got the feeling they were laughing about me. Tina didn't seem to mind at all when I had to go away for another six-week tour, though I was heartsick. She called me a milksop.

One day, when we were travelling to a gig in Hamilton, Rick pulled the bus off the Desert Road and drew up outside Rangipo Prison, where Graeme Nesbitt was nearing the end of an eighteen-month lag. It was his second spell of imprisonment, again for selling pot to cover the shortfall from a Dragon venture. While serving his earlier sentence he had been joined for a few months by Rick. The way Rick described it, it didn't sound all that different from the times they'd flatted together in Aro Valley. Sharing a cell, they discovered that between them they could recite from memory the entirety of Shakespeare's *Hamlet*. They also formed a band with other prisoners, calling it Rick and The Rock Breakers.

Rick went in to see Graeme while the rest of us waited. Although it was a minimum security prison, I was surprised when Graeme wandered casually into the yard where the bus was parked, said hello and wished us luck. He looked healthy and tanned, and amused to see Rick with a fresh busload of disciples.

If he were not in prison, Graeme might have been managing Rough Justice, using his charm and cunning to secure us better gigs. In the absence of a manager the task had fallen to Rick, which in those pre-cellphone days meant parking the bus somewhere near a phone booth and emptying our pockets for change so he could call ahead to confirm our next booking. Rick did not enjoy communicating with publicans. He marvelled at bandleaders who simply treated it as part of the job. They might tell a joke, say something about the rugby, maybe even have a drink with the bar manager after the gig. He knew that this often gained them better fees and more frequent bookings but it was not in his nature to schmooze. I would see Rick through the glass of the phone booth, negotiating through gritted teeth.

He had a small network of contacts who sometimes found us gigs. He referred to them as promoters but they were usually characters he had met in prison: honest, good-hearted people but not natural entrepreneurs. One was Arney, who booked us several nights' work either side of New Year in a gigantic gymnasium in Mount Maunganui. The place turned out to be approximately a thousand times too large for the number of people who showed up to hear us, but at least we didn't have to pay for accommodation: Arney had given us the run of his rural homestead.

During the days of that summer residency we'd sleep, swim at the nearby beach, help Janet with the ongoing task of painting the bus, and argue over the set list. Our final night drew our biggest crowd, a few dozen locals. Next morning we packed the bus and went to farewell Arney but he had already left town, heading for the Kaimai Ranges. His message said he was going to work on the construction of New Zealand's longest railway tunnel until he had paid off the debts incurred by his venture into music promotion.

The bus had by now undergone several expensive repairs, and I had begun to wonder if it was false economy to travel this way. It was hard to calculate the bus's value as a publicity device. When we drove down the main street of any small town – often several times in succession as one of us studied the map and Rick tried to remember the address of the venue – people would stare as though at a giant moving billboard or passing circus. But the bus also made us highly visible to the police. We were stopped frequently. Usually they just wanted to check that our warrant and registration were compliant and we had paid our road user charges, but the more zealous often had a sniff around as well. The first time we were busted we were driving between Titirangi and our Ponsonby crash pad. It was late at night. We had been to visit Ian Watkin, the former Blerta member. He had cooked us a lavish dinner, far better than any road food or pub fare, plied us with wine, and regaled us with his own road tales, such as the time the Brisbane drug squad had descended backstage before a Blerta concert and searched his bag for contraband. They had found only his Cricket Umpires' Association badge, and this had distracted them long enough for the rest of the band to sneak off and dispose of their stash.

As the police signalled us to pull over, Rick stubbed out his joint. Boyd had a tiny amount of pot in his pocket. He and Rick were taken to the police station. It was Rick's tenth bust but Boyd's first. Rick took responsibility for the pot and used his allotted phone call to ring Boyd's partner in Wellington and

warn her that a search of her property might ensue. She was half asleep and Rick was talking in code. 'Ah, hi Bern, we've had some trouble with the bus. It's the usual thing but don't worry, Boyd's okay, it's just small bananas.' The next morning she was still wondering about the bananas.

By 1979 Rough Justice had begun to draw bigger crowds in the cities and we were starting to build a following at the Gluepot, the Ponsonby pub favoured by Hello Sailor and Street Talk. But our most appreciative audiences continued to be far from the cities with their hungover hoteliers and urbane critics. In the early '70s some of Rick's contemporaries – dropouts he had known from the Duke and university days – had left Wellington with dreams of living off the land. During Labour's brief term in office from 1972 to 1975, there had even been state support for such moves, with Prime Minister Norman Kirk overseeing the establishment of the ohu scheme. Under this, remote areas of Crown land were made available for the establishment of communes, a possible antidote to what political historian Margaret Hayward called 'the ills of modern society, as well as a means of showing people the virtues of a simpler life'. Other people pooled resources and bought land of their own. Community halls in tiny townships on the Coromandel Peninsula or the West Coast of the South Island became a kind of tribal meeting place for some of these groups.

When we visited such communities, rustic revolutionaries in richly coloured clothes would come out of the hills to hear us. There would be none of the usual blank stares, or moans of 'Play something we can dance to.' From the first note, these occasions would be big benign bacchanals, with Rick at his most relaxed. The happiest I ever saw him on stage was one night in a community hall at Barrytown, population 225. He commanded centre stage, a large joint in his mouth, which he removed only to sing. Standing behind him with the lights in my eyes, all I could see was a giant cloud of smoke.

20
SHOWDOWN AT THE SPECTRUM BAR

Whenever Rough Justice were back in Wellington our favourite place to play was a café above Courtenay Place called the Last Resort. We had to lug our heavy equipment up a steep flight of stairs, and the fee was dependent on the door take, but it was the rare venue where we were not forced to negotiate with angry alcoholic publicans and drunk dissatisfied customers, or tortured with a siren at the end of the evening. We had a dressing room. We got free Cona coffee, and carrot cake with cream.

The reason the Last Resort was musician-friendly was simple: it was run by musicians. Clinton Brown, the bass player for Rockinghorse, had launched the venue in 1978 after his band experienced problems with publicans. Just two years earlier Rockinghorse had been the best group in New Zealand, with an award to prove it. RATA, the Recording Arts Talent Awards, had been introduced in 1973 to replace the Loxene Golden Disc Awards, a national institution since the 1960s. Rockinghorse had won in November 1975 for their single 'Through the Southern Moonlight'. The award had been presented to them by visiting

British-based American rocker Suzi Quatro, dressed in her customary leathers, in an afternoon ceremony at Television New Zealand's Lower Hutt studios. After the formalities, the champagne had started flowing and the members of Rockinghorse, chuffed with their success, had partaken freely. It was early evening before someone remembered the band had a booking that night.

The gig was at the Spectrum Bar. Rockinghorse often played there when they weren't busy at the EMI recording studios. In the past year, as well as recording an album of their own and the aforementioned hit, they had provided the backing on records by Mark Williams, Prince Tui Teka and The Yandall Sisters, all popular Māori and Samoan singers who were among the country's biggest-selling recording acts. They had also toured nationally, mostly on the Lion Breweries circuit. There can't have been a harder-working band in the country. But it had not escaped the musicians' notice that for all their efforts none of them were getting rich. The breweries, meanwhile, were prospering.

Rockinghorse were known for their tight country-rock groove and warm harmonies. Not surprisingly, their performance at Spectrum that night was less polished than usual. The band was a drunken mess, and at the end of the night the bar manager, Brian Foster, told them so. Emboldened by bubbly, singer Carl Evensen reminded him they were the best band in the country with a RATA to prove it, and told him what he could do with his gig. Next morning the bass player, Clinton Brown, was woken by a call from Alan Galbraith, house producer for EMI. He'd just got off the phone with Richard Holden, who had rung to inform him that Rockinghorse were banned from the Breweries circuit and would not be welcome in any Lion venue again. The message was clear: bands had to know their place. Rockinghorse might be the best but Lion was the biggest.

For a while Rockinghorse tried to brazen out the blacklisting. They still had the EMI contract, and the RATA had to be good for something. In April 1976 they released their second album, *Grand Affaire*, but over the following months the reality of their situation dawned on them. There were only a few places they could play: the occasional school ball, the even more occasional rock festival, and a few taverns not operated by Lion. But the golden age of EMI was coming to an end, with an increasingly commercial and competitive radio market turning its back on locally recorded music. Rockinghorse would not make another record.

Starved of gigs but inspired by a visit to Charley Gray's Island of Real, Clinton Brown concluded that the only way to achieve autonomy was to start his own venue, so with his friend Kerry Simpson, who had worked in real estate and had a small amount of capital to invest, he opened the aptly named Last Resort. A rejuvenated Rockinghorse played the first night. Recent addition Steve Garden – one of the original Rough Justice members whom Rick had left at the roadside – had a lot to do with it. Garden's drumming and Brown's basslines locked into a rolling groove. Guitarist Kevin Bayley was similarly inspired, snapping and twanging, especially on great songs of his own like 'Julia' and 'Danny's Blues'. It was as though someone had left the gate open and the horse had bolted.

Ironically, by the time Last Resort opened, the Lion pubs would probably have been ready to receive Rockinghorse again. The two main protagonists in the Spectrum Bar showdown had moved on. Evensen left Rockinghorse in 1978, around the time

Holden took on a new role as Lion's head of exports. Holden's departure could be seen as symbolic. The era of the salaried showbands that he had overseen was gradually drawing to a close as the number of bands bringing original music into pubs – and getting away with it – was growing.

Back in the mid '70s a few groups had tried, with some success, to present their own material. Dunedin's Mother Goose had done well in the South Island, particularly at Shoreline Hotel in their hometown and Aranui Hotel in Christchurch, with a brand of vaudeville rock that involved elaborate dress-ups: each member of the all-male band had his own persona – ballerina, mouse, sailor, pixie, baby, bee. But within a year of their formation Mother Goose had decamped to Australia.

Ragnarok, Think and Schtung – from Auckland, Hamilton and Wellington respectively – had all tested varieties of prog on pub-goers. Yet even with two albums of ambitious originals, Ragnarok had been forced by popular demand to augment their own material with Led Zeppelin and Peter Frampton covers, while Think's set included an entire side of Pink Floyd's *Dark Side of the Moon*. These forward-thinking groups soon retreated to the more welcoming world of campus and small theatre concerts before being defeated by sheer economics.

It was around the same time that Hello Sailor started playing the pubs. At first the only gig they could find was a Monday night at Kiwi Tavern, across the road from the Auckland University campus. Their first trip out of town, booked by Mike Corless, took them to Tokoroa's Trees Tavern and Napier's Leopard Inn. They too peppered their set with well-known covers – Steely Dan and Thin Lizzy songs – but their hearts were in their increasingly convincing originals. By the time Rough Justice got on the road with our eclectic set of R&B covers, Corless was at last starting to get some traction with this new breed of original rock group, drawing the kind of numbers that paid off. Meanwhile, former drawcards of the pub circuit such as The Constellations and Maori Volcanics were heading overseas: they could make better money in places like Australia's Gold Coast.

New Zealand's live music scene was changing, but where Rough Justice might fit into the new order barely crossed our minds. We were just trying to survive from gig to gig, wondering whether our next meal would be pig's head or carrot cake.

21
PUNKS AND INDEPENDENTS

It's nearly forty years now since Charley Gray burst into Rough Justice's crash pad, barking about how someone had covered up his posters. His voice still has the same abrasive timbre and his sentences issue forth in rapid staccato bursts, like paradiddles on a snare drum. 'A lot of people don't seem to like me,' he says, and glares, as though challenging me to side with them. But as he tells his story in a Ponsonby Road café it strikes me there is something admirable, even noble, about this sprightly silver-haired septuagenarian. Almost sixty years after he entered the business he is as enthusiastic as ever about music, despite having little material wealth to show for a life of passion.

Charley had been a drummer for almost twenty years when he opened Island of Real in 1977; he still practises drums four to five hours a day. His first professional gig was with Howard Morrison, three months of one-nighters from North Cape to Bluff, but his real love was jazz. From 1962 to 1964 he was in London, playing in the experimental jazz scene. By the mid '70s he was back in Auckland, working as a warehouseman to support his wife, Anne, and their three children. One night he splashed out and took Anne to dinner at La Boheme, Auckland's oldest and most upmarket restaurant. 'We ate beautiful food and watched beautiful people and we'd never really done anything like that before, and I just thought, this is a whole different lifestyle. I came from a working-class background. In fact my father's only advice to me as father to son was, "You're working class, don't ever forget it. You vote Labour, that's it." I thought, different bloody lifestyle and we're down below it. We needed to do something to break out of the poverty thing.'

Charley and Anne found an empty printing factory in downtown Auckland, and with $3,000 borrowed from Charley's sister the couple fitted it out as a performance café. It opened in early 1977. The front half was for food and coffee; the filled rolls were legendary. The performance area was at the back, curtained off. Initially the Island of Real Café focused on fringe theatrical events. 'I liked doing experimental things,' Charley tells me. 'It just appealed. I had this fantasy of a groovy type of venue with a stage and some lights, where people could do unusual stuff and we could make enough money to have a holiday once a year. I think we managed that once.'

An early booking was expatriate Californian multimedia artist Frank Womble. 'I was helping Anne out the front, the kids were watching, and they came running up and said, "Dad, he's taking his clothes off!" I go and have a look and he's bollock naked. I don't know what he was doing; it was just part of the show.'

Gradually, the bands started coming. After Th' Dudes played there on several occasions they approached Charley about his becoming their manager. 'I knocked them back a couple of times

The Island of Real

and my wife said to me, "Don't be bloody silly, you could do great things for those guys and it would be good for you too."'

For a band of aspiring stars fuelled by youthful arrogance, Charley was the ideal manager. Older, authoritative and ferocious, he acted as a buffer between Th' Dudes and the rest of the world, enabling them to become the stars they already imagined they were. When a major summer festival offered the group a paltry $400, telling Charley that every other top band in the country was taking the same fee as the 'exposure' would be invaluable, he told them that, with Th' Dudes' third single currently at No. 1, the band hardly needed any more exposure. He immediately booked the Dunedin Town Hall and Th' Dudes filled it to capacity, as they had every other venue along the way.

He also battled the breweries. By 1978 the Gluepot – Dominion Breweries' Ponsonby Club Hotel – was Auckland's most celebrated rock venue. Bands like Street Talk, Hello Sailor, Th' Dudes and even Rough Justice would draw capacity crowds. Charley proposed to the manager, Les Wilson, that he raise the two-dollar cover charge by 50 cents. When Wilson refused, arguing it would mean 50 cents less that customers would be spending across his bar, Th' Dudes staged a boycott, shifting to the Station Hotel less than a kilometre away, where they drew upwards of 600 people a night.

Th' Dudes' success represented the marriage of a band determined to be heard on its own terms and a giant industry whose goal was to keep people drinking beer, agendas that had often seemed irreconcilable in the past. The achievement was encapsulated with irony in one of their most successful songs.

'Bliss', an original by Dudes guitarists Dave Dobbyn and Ian Morris, had a pulsating riff and singalong chorus. It might have started out as a cynical parody of the drinking culture but it quickly became the ultimate drinking anthem. Decades later *Drink yourself more bliss* and the refrain *Ya ya ya ya ya* still echo in rugby stadiums.

Charley Gray continued to host adventurous and original bands at Island of Real. Neither it nor Last Resort served alcohol: they couldn't get a licence. In the early '60s – against the opposition of a powerful lobby that included Alcoholics Anonymous, the Salvation Army and the breweries – a handful of high-end restaurants had finally been granted the right to serve wine and beer, but the Licensing Control Commission had continued to maintain a strict set of conditions that these independent music venues were unable to meet.

Clinton Brown tells me of the lengths to which he and Kerry Simpson went to try and get a limited licence for Last Resort. They invited the head of the Licensing Control Commission to lunch. It was a gorgeous day. Sunlight was streaming through the windows and Last Resort was looking its best. All they wanted, they explained to the commissioner, was to be able to sell a glass of wine or beer with meals. They weren't interested in selling spirits. His reply was blunt. 'First of all, you can't get a licence like that. You're either fully licensed or you're not.' He then checked out the premises – toilets, kitchen – and announced they would have to spend between $15,000 and $20,000 on refurbishments before a licence would be considered 'and even then there's no guarantee you'll get one'.

'The thought of spending twenty grand on spec was out of the question,' Clinton says. 'If we could have managed that it might have kept the business going. You couldn't survive on orange juice, cakes and Cona coffee. That was the power the breweries had, of course. They didn't want anyone else getting licences. All that power and money. We were just the little guys, trying to do our best.'

If laws favouring the beer barons made it hard for these venues, the changing nature of the crowds wasn't helping either. Punk had emerged as a cult movement in Britain some time during 1976, challenging the sense of entitlement displayed by many rock stars still around from the '60s. But it was a March 1977 episode of the local television current affairs programme *Eyewitness* that thrust punk into the eyeballs of New Zealand. Reporting from London, television journalist Dylan Taite presented an item that intercut video of the Sex Pistols' incendiary 'Anarchy in the UK' with snippets of nihilistic rhetoric from an assortment of young British punks and, in a journalistic coup, an interview with Pistols' frontman Johnny Rotten, conducted outside Buckingham Palace.

Soon local punks began to appear. Not long after I had joined Rough Justice I bumped into a guy I had known at Onslow. There he had been a benign longhair. Now his hair was short and spiked, he was wearing stovepipe tartan trousers and spitting emphatically on the footpath at the ends of sentences. He told me he was starting a band. He was going to be the bass player.

While Rough Justice were in the South Island on our first tour, punk had come to Wellington. The Scavengers and Suburban

Reptiles, Auckland's first two punk bands, had played a Students Arts Festival show at the Union Hall. My friends were still talking about it when we got back a week later. The Reptiles' drummer had thrown a drumstick into the audience and hit a girl in the eye. Her boyfriend had jumped onstage and hit somebody with a guitar. It all sounded wild and chaotic. What had the music been like? A bit rough seemed to be the consensus, but no one could tell me much about it.

As punk proliferated, its agenda varied from band to band. Some bands were overtly political and wrote earnest angry songs about society's ills. Some were carnival anarchists. Some were essentially covers bands with a punk bias. In Auckland punk soon had its own venue, Zwines. In Wellington punks took over what had formerly been Chez Paree, one of the capital's famous folk clubs, painted the walls black and renamed it The Mindshaft. A building behind Trades Hall, operating as Rock Theatre, would sometimes host punk acts too.

Punk needed an enemy and found plenty. Sometimes that enemy was the existing music scene, which it saw as boring, elitist and – worst of all – run by hippies. Although Last Resort booked few punk bands, its reputation didn't keep the punks away. Clinton Brown recalls the afternoon a local punk came to warn him that a minivan full of punks was on its way from Auckland with the express purpose of creating havoc in Wellington. 'I thought, Jesus, we've only got one bouncer.' The warning was timely. The punks turned up and roared through the door. 'We had a bowl of cream on the counter for the coffee and a guy immediately grabbed it and started firing cream everywhere. They were cutting themselves. It was a nightmare.'

DOMINION

THURSDAY, AUGUST 25, 1977

PIQUED PUNK ROCK POPSTER HURTS GIRL

Charley Gray remembers Anne once finding a young female punk systematically demolishing the toilet bowl with a hammer. It sometimes seemed the punks made no distinction between monopolist breweries and noble independents such as Clinton and Charley: all were representations of some vague oppressive 'other'. But it's not hard to see how exclusive and complacent the beard-and-flares brigade must have seemed. Punk, by comparison, was a club to which anyone could belong.

At a party not long ago I found myself describing the subject of this book to a man I had just met. Three or four years younger than me, he was slightly drunk, the stereo was loud and I wasn't sure how well he could hear me, but he sprang to life at the mention of Last Resort.

'That was the first live music venue I ever went to!' he shouted. 'I must have been fourteen or fifteen. My mates and I came in from the Hutt to see what this famous Wellington music scene was all about. What a disappointment. The cover charge was steep – at least five dollars – and the band was playing this very old-school rhythm and blues. A sea of flared denim. Some of them even had beards. There was a guy playing saxophone. God it was boring. They were called Rough Justice.'

'Ah yes, I think I remember that band,' I deadpanned as he ranted on. A few weeks later he had gone back again, only this time the door charge was lower and the band unknown. Their name was The Ambitious Vegetables and they were his kind of group: young, bratty, irreverent, plenty of attitude.

I thought of how, like him, my schoolmates and I had gone in search of music just a few years earlier. What we had found had been the sound of possibilities, of fighting back against the forces of the establishment, the beginning of something. That was what The Ambitious Vegetables had represented for this man. As for Rough Justice, a band that included one or more of the musicians who had blown my teenage mind: what did we represent in 1979?

22
GONEVILLE

Whitewashed breeze-block walls. Sunlight pushing at the edges of a closed curtain. A half glass of water on a bedside table. An open suitcase on the floor, clothes spilling out. A bass guitar propped against a chair. Where am I? It would be easier to figure that out if these surroundings, or the gig we played last night, stood out from any other of these past two years.

It had been a small crowd for a Friday, or was it a Thursday? A few customers had come as far as the door but backed away when confronted with the two-dollar cover charge. During the second set someone had shouted, 'Can't you play anything decent?' Towards the end of the third set, after we'd been going almost three hours, a couple of girls had got up to dance to 'Don't Leave Me This Way', the disco song. It's always the disco song. A few guys had followed them on to the dancefloor and flung themselves around for the last few minutes of the set. When Rick announced the final song the boys slunk back to their beers and the girls said, 'Whaddaya mean? We've only just got here. You can't stop yet. Jeez, what a slack band.'

Rick had thanked the crowd for coming and reminded them we'd be back the next night, and the bar manager had turned on the merciless fluoro lights to let everyone know it was eleven p.m. and time to go, wherever they liked, he didn't care but they couldn't stay here. And after a few more minutes, while people were draining their glasses and asking where the party was, he had switched on the siren to drive the last of them from the room. This was common practice in many of the bars we played. We would often have to suffer the tinnitus-inducing noise until we'd packed away our instruments.

I pull back the flowery drapes and notice the bus is no longer in the forecourt, which means Rick has gone into town with some of the others in search of breakfast. I put on some clothes and go down the corridor to check the rest of the rooms. Rick's door is locked, which confirms that he's out. Same with Boyd's and Martin's. Peter and Mike are both still asleep.

Unsure which direction leads to town, I set off on foot for nowhere in particular, down wide flat footpaths with grassy berms, past squat wooden houses with tiled roofs and neatly fenced front lawns. Did any of last night's crowd go home to these places? It's hard to picture those people in these houses. I pass three churches and two petrol stations, and the occasional car passes me, but I don't see any faces and everywhere feels empty and abandoned. I walk for maybe half an hour and the houses get closer together, although I can't tell whether I'm getting any nearer to breakfast. Another half a mile and the road becomes a bridge and soon I'm standing above a wide river with thick native bush along both banks. I am drawn, as though magnetised, to the steel railing. I lean over, look down into the deep olive-black water and have the crazy thought that everyone in this town just came here, jumped in and disappeared.

It is two years since I boarded the Rough Justice bus and headed south on our first tour. In a fortnight we'll be home in Wellington, but only for a few nights. Rick's booked us another month on the road after that. Recently we were playing in Rotorua, in an old wooden hotel that had seen few refurbishments since it was built in the 1920s. We stayed in upstairs guest rooms with creaky single beds. The ground floor was a maze of corridors and bars. There was no stage in the lounge bar but we had found a couple of extra lights to illuminate our area of the floor so we weren't looking too shabby. By nine p.m. a dozen people were seated shyly around the darker corners of the room as we worked through our rock and soul covers. We had recently added a Betty Wright song, 'Clean Up Woman', to the repertoire, and I loved dropping those deep bass notes into the pockets between Martin's kick drum and the clickety guitar licks.

In the break before the last set I took an aimless stroll around the hotel. In the corridor I could hear a muffled thrum. I followed the sound until I reached an internal door. It opened into the public bar. Suddenly I was in a big, brightly lit room, on the edge of a throng of people. There was an equal number of men and women and everyone was singing with joy and abandon. Among the tables and chairs, seated on a bar stool with a jug of beer on a high table in front of him, was a middle-aged Māori man strumming an acoustic guitar and leading the chorus: 'Oh, hula, a-hula, a-hula to my ten guitars …'

It's not the only time lately I've wondered if our band is surplus to requirements. In Christchurch a hundred people had crammed into a brick and concrete warehouse where we were sharing a bill with a couple of newer groups. First up had been a punk trio, The Vauxhalls. Their songs were mostly their own, none lasted more than two minutes, and Edison would have envied their energy. Then it was our turn. We opened with 'In the Midnight Hour', a reliable R&B classic with honking saxophones that seldom failed to get crowds going, but after The Vauxhalls it sounded sombre and slow. The song that went down best that night was 'Take Me to the River'. In the eighteen months since we learned this obscure Al Green song it had been covered on a hit album by the post-punk band Talking Heads, so now most people thought we were playing a Talking Heads tune.

I could see the noncommittal expressions as the crowd took in our sound and appearance, trying to figure out what we represented and whether they had any use for it. At least Rick always made an impression. In his sleeveless jean jacket with the Rough Justice gang patch Janet had painted and sewn on the back, he could pass, if not for a punk, then as suitably anti-establishment. And Boyd, a snappy dresser since the days of his pink velvet pants, has taken to wearing seersucker suits. He inhabits a world and fashion sense of his own. But the rest of us, with our denim, long hair, occasional beard or moustache, may have stepped off the cover of a 1976 Doobie Brothers album, which in 1979 is not a good thing. I am twenty, no older than most of the punks and younger than some of them, yet I feel like a weary veteran.

The bus, like the band, is becoming a symbol of a bygone age, a psychedelic relic alongside the air-conditioned coaches more successful bands tour in. Whenever the band earns any money, the bus suffers another breakdown and consumes it all. In Kaikoura we were stuck for three days as we waited for the arrival of a new differential. It was midwinter and with no budget for accommodation we had to stay aboard the bus, parked outside the local mechanic's shop, playing cards in our sleeping bags. On another occasion our vehicle spluttered to a standstill on State Highway One, just out of Amberley. While we were wondering what to do, a farmer heading south stopped to see what the problem was. 'So you'll be wanting to get to Christchurch then?' We arrived in Christchurch towed by a tractor, like a tattered float in an A&P show.

Of the other bands that were on the road when Rough Justice started out, most have either broken through or broken up. Not long ago Hello Sailor, Th' Dudes, Citizen Band and Street Talk were all playing the same provincial pubs as us, slipping in a few of their original songs among covers the crowds would recognise. Now they all have records out. Last year I'd seen Hello Sailor headlining at the Opera House in Wellington. Graham Brazier strode the stage as though marking out his territory, the audience's attention feeding him like a drug. Since then the band have gone to Los Angeles, seeking success commensurate with their swagger. And the Red Mole Theatre Troupe have decamped to New York, taking some of the Country Flyers with them.

As for Rough Justice, we have finally begun to get work in some of the Lion pubs. But the fact we are now welcome in these venues, once fiercely controlled by Richard Holden, is just another measure of how times have changed. The legendary Lion contracts that would once have given each member of the band a weekly wage no longer exist. Instead, we are booked for two or three nights a week for a percentage of the door take, leaving us no better off than we ever were.

The campus circuit has also changed. It has ceased to be the door to a countercultural playground, with the kind of underground happenings Graeme Nesbitt once presided over. When we arrive to play at a student arts festival, the organisers who greet us look like commerce students. No one has a light show like Peter Frater's any more. It's as if the worlds I had glimpsed at the beginning of the decade – the campus underground and the pub circuit – had been mirages in a desert, creations of light and imagination that vanished just as they seemed within reach.

Janet has given up travelling with the band. She is preparing to go to art school and is back in Wellington working on her portfolio. We have acquired a longhaired, often shirtless roadie called Mal, who doubles as sound mixer and bus driver. It is useful to have another person who can deputise for Rick at the wheel and keep an ear on our temperamental sound system. Mal has added some duties of his own; they include each night introducing himself to as many of the women in the bar as possible.

One night a high squeal begins in one of the stage monitors. As it grows in intensity I look towards the mixing desk in the middle of the room, expecting to see Mal hunched over the faders, furiously seeking out the offending frequency, but his seat is empty. As the feedback increases to an ear-splitting howl, I spot a familiar head of shoulder-length hair at the back of the room. It's Mal, an arm draped around a female shoulder. 'Mal!' Rick summons sternly into his mic. It seems to take a few moments for Mal to recognise his name, by which time members of the audience are clasping their hands to their ears. Mal glances towards the bandstand, gives a cheery wave, mouths encouragement – 'Sounding great!' – and returns to the matter at hand.

The musical line-up has been growing too. Dennis Mason, who had played in The Quincy Conserve, has joined on saxophone, which means we now have a horn section. We have also recruited Tony Backhouse, formerly of Mammal, with his stratospheric vocals and quirky original songs. One of these songs requires us to sing the inscrutable chorus 'Maybe the Goneville line is down'.

As usual, Rick calculates that these additions will, at some unspecified point in the future, increase our earning power. While Tony's excellent but challenging material draws a generally blank response from the provincial crowds, it wins us a touch of critical credibility in the cities. But he is only passing through. Fane Flaws, who has been in Blerta, is incubating a new band that will wrap his love of Zappa and psychedelic Beatles in the New Wave trappings of Blondie, Devo and Elvis Costello, and will include Tony, along with Bruno Lawrence. Fane has already thought of a name, The Crocodiles, and had a vision in which he has seen it on a Top 20 playlist alongside a song title, 'Tears'. Soon he and Arthur Baysting will get around to writing the song. Tony has warned us he'll be leaving Rough Justice towards the end of the year to work on The Crocodiles' first album.

Rough Justice hasn't made any records. With the exception of a few proven commercial hitmakers, or persuasive visionaries such as Fane Flaws, the doors of the record companies are closed to local bands, especially now the sales tax is so high and the radio stations are beginning to import their playlists and programmers from overseas. What's more, we are still essentially a covers band, even if the covers we play are only the songs we love, not necessarily the ones pub crowds want to hear.

There is no obvious way for the group to advance itself, yet Rick hardly seems bothered as long as the bus is overloaded with band gear, the petrol gauge shows half a tank, and we are on a state highway headed for another gig. The road, I realise, is where Rick is happiest. On the road, time is suspended. There is no one to hold you to account. You are always on your way somewhere. But I start to imagine I'll look out one day from the window of the bus and find the road has run out, that we have driven into the middle of nowhere and there is no way back.

I carry on walking until I am at the other side of the bridge, getting closer to what must be the centre of this provincial New Zealand town with the name I can't remember but think of as Goneville. I don't want breakfast. I want to go home.

23
OFF THE BUS

As it turned out I wasn't the only one thinking about getting off the bus. Mike had been making plans to go to the Sydney Conservatorium of Music to study jazz. Boyd and Martin were entertaining similar thoughts. Peter had fallen in love with a Swiss Italian woman and was considering a move to Europe. Tony would be leaving soon to become a full-time Crocodile. We discussed our plans over pitiful coffees in a Whangarei tea room one afternoon between the soundcheck and the gig. Rick was back at the venue, still tinkering with the sound system.

There was probably no such thing as a good time to tell Rick we were all leaving, but there couldn't have been a worse one than just before that night's show. After Mike broke the news, Rick sang the entire set without making eye contact with any of us. He didn't leave us stranded at the roadside like the previous line-up, but the next day he drove the entire 800 kilometres back to Wellington in stoned silence.

We still had a few bookings left to honour. I feared these nights would be as bleak as the one in Whangarei. Yet without the endless road in front of us, making music unexpectedly became fun again. Knowing these were the last times I'd ever play those basslines behind Rick's voice, every note felt finite, and more powerful for it. After ignoring us for two years, the Wellington commercial radio station 2ZM made Rough Justice its Band of the Month. That gave us a couple of days of free studio time, and we recorded four originals. We would be leaving our handprint on the cave wall of Kiwi rock.

While we had been away on one of our tours, Tina and Sally and their friend Andrea had decided to form a band. They had watched us rehearse, and get gigs and even audiences. How hard could it be? One obstacle was a lack of instruments or equipment but they could always borrow ours. Andrea knew some chords. She tried them out on Stephen's Stratocaster and quickly became a passable rhythm guitarist. I showed Tina a couple of basslines on my old Höfner and within days she was figuring out her own parts. They had heard about a schoolteacher from Hamilton who had recently moved to Wellington and was keen to sing, and asked her to join. Her name was Jenny Morris. Sally was the drummer. She had never played drums before but Bruno Lawrence offered her a lesson. One of the first songs in the repertoire of the Wide Mouthed Frogs (as they named themselves) was 'Do the Blue Beat', Dinah Lee's big Australasian hit of the 1960s. Sally asked Bruno if he could show her what the drummer on the record was doing. Bruno said he should be able to: he'd played on the original.

When they had half a dozen songs ready, The Wide Mouthed Frogs were ready to face the crowds. Rough Justice agreed to let them play an opening set at Rock Theatre in Vivian Street. They

caused a storm. There were then few women in bands doing anything other than singing. Here, for the first time as far as most audiences were concerned, was a group of women doing it all – singing, playing, the lot. Their choice of covers was simple and appealing. There were no gratuitous solos; no song outstayed its welcome. They were funny, irreverent and loved being on the stage. When they opened for us again a few weeks later, the venue operators, sensing who the real drawcard was, reversed the billing in the newspaper ad. Now it was WIDE-MOUTHED FROGS – ALL GIRL BAND! 'Rough Justice' appeared in tiny type below.

Soon the Frogs were off on a national tour. And they had a manager: Graeme Nesbitt. When Graeme was released from prison I had wondered whether he might take on the management of Rough Justice, but his appetite for bands in brightly painted buses seemed to have faded. In an ironic reversal, I would soon be at home in Wellington reading letters from the road by Tina and Sally.

The Frogs seemed to be having a far more glamorous touring experience than Rough Justice ever had. *Well this is the life*, began one of Tina's letters. *Lying on our beds writing letters and watching colour TV, and drinking gins and tonics, mid-afternoon, feeling refreshed and wonderful after lying in the sun all afternoon and going for swims in the swimming pool directly outside the door …*

Sally wrote: A *fun day in Gisborne on Sunday – did an outdoor concert with a couple of local bands and a really mad poet, and Bruno and his kids turned up having chartered an aeroplane to get there … Graeme reckons it's the best tour he's ever been on.*

Rough Justice played our final gig at Rock Theatre on July 26, 1979. Arthur Baysting, in his Neville Purvis guise, was MC. Bill Lake led The Windy City Strugglers in a typically shambolic set, and The Wide Mouthed Frogs performed an item they had worked up especially for the occasion:

(To the tune of 'The Sound of Music')
The hills are alive with the sound of Rough boys
With songs they have sung
For a thousand years
Their songs fill our hearts
With the sound of music
We still want to sing every song we hear

Farewell to Mike and Martin
To Steve and Nick
To Peter and Boyd and lastly farewell to Rick
When he leaps in the air and trips and falls
Over leads on the stage
And knocks Martin's drums, who stands up
And walks off in a rage

We go hear the Roughs when our hearts are lonely
We know we will hear what we've heard before
And we go see the Roughs when we want to practise
And now we can't any more

We'll miss their amps and their speakers, their drums and leads
Their mikes and their horns

Their P.A. and desk, but what will make us forlorn
Is knowing the Roughs are no longer with us
They who have done more than words can say
Have been forced to disband due to personal problems
And a lack of pay.

Early one evening, not long before that farewell show, I had gone to collect some equipment I'd left at Willy's Wine Bar, a subterranean pub in central Wellington where an after-work office crowd would sit around tables, talk loudly and ignore the musicians. As I descended the stairs I could hear a magnificent din above the chatter. It was a new band from Auckland. I hadn't heard Toy Love before, although I'd met a few of them one night with Rough Justice at an Uncle's takeaway bar on Karangahape Road, where we had stopped on our way home from respective gigs. One of them, who turned out to be bass player Paul Kean, had asked, 'So which band are you?'

Kean and the keyboard player, Jane Walker, had been in a band in Christchurch called The Basket Cases. The other three came from The Enemy, Dunedin's first punk band, which had moved to Auckland and promptly broken up. With Alec Bathgate's trebly guitar and Walker's piercing electric keyboard sounding like something off an old La De Da's record, they could almost have beamed down from The Galaxie circa 1967. The main thing that identified them as a product of the punk era and not some '60s teleport was singer Chris Knox.

Knox, at twenty-six, was possibly the country's oldest punk. He stalked the edge of the stage, microphone in hand, surveying with mischievous intent an audience who, with a few exceptions,

seemed to be a typical, conservatively dressed Willy's crowd. Then he jumped off the stage to prowl among the tables, leaning inches from the faces of startled drinkers, serenading them like a demented supper-club crooner. Unsatisfied with the reaction, he picked up a broken beer glass and, his grin nearly splitting his face in two, stabbed himself in the forehead, splattering blood over askance office workers. It was shocking, yet unexpectedly and overwhelmingly uplifting. Knox was determined to connect at any cost. When he sang of *sex, drugs and rock 'n' roll, huddled together in a bottomless hole* he was not celebrating nihilism, but rather renouncing the self-destruction with which rock 'n' roll seemed to have blighted itself.

Among their spectacular originals, Toy Love scattered a few songs that I wouldn't have expected to hear any band play, anywhere. They did an astonishing version of The Doors' 'People Are Strange'. Better still was a medley of Bob Dylan's 'Positively 4th Street' and The Ohio Express's 'Yummy Yummy Yummy', combining with perfect absurdity one of the most bitter, deep-versed songs of the '60s with one of the most cheerfully inane.

The decade was coming to an end. So was the band I had been playing in for two years, along with the vague dream I'd had of making a living playing the music I loved. But at that moment New Zealand rock 'n' roll could not have seemed more furiously alive.

24
TRENDY LEFTIES AND ORDINARY BLOKES

There were times during the '70s when it felt to me as though the love of music that had stung me as a child was the only constant thing in my life. And yet during those years music had changed too, reshaped by fashion, and forces even greater. At the start of the decade there had been a profound division between the music served as entertainment on New Zealand television and radio and the music I had found at the Union Hall and elsewhere. The former was the music of the mainstream, songs everybody knew. The latter was, for want of a better term, the music of the counterculture. It was a secret soundtrack, broadcasting on its own underground frequency. When Bruno Lawrence directed Blerta's anarchic extravaganzas from behind his ragtag drum kit, or Mammal sang 'Play Nasty for Me' while Peter Frater's lights painted their faces in lurid shades, you were either there in the room, experiencing the event in all its dimensions – sonically, visually, bodily – or knew nothing of it at all. You couldn't hear it on the radio or see it on television, let alone watch it on YouTube, download it as a podcast, or access it via any of the other media that today allow us to sample, in vicarious and diluted ways, a little of everything.

The music that made it to the airwaves back then was crafted for a different purpose and different people. Listening now to the local pop records of the early '70s, I'm impressed by how well made so many of them are – something that, as a teenage rock snob, I would have been loath to acknowledge. Māori singers such as Mark Williams, Bunny Walters and Prince Tui Teka, many backed in the studio by Rockinghorse, created what now strikes me as a type of indigenous soul music, albeit one influenced more by Nashville country and Italian aria than by James Brown. Once on the East Cape I heard Prince Tui Teka's 'Mum' playing while singleted labourers shot pool and drank beer by the jug. I'm not sure anyone actually sang along, but someone had put a coin in the jukebox to hear the song and I could tell it was appreciated. Suddenly its social function seemed absolutely clear. The mother in Prince Tui's song was the mother of every man in the room. She might be alive or dead, it didn't matter. By celebrating her life Teka had given her a presence in that bar, so she could remind her sons that however drunk they got, whoever won the pool or the rugby, whomever they got into a fight with, they should never forget the responsibilities they had to their wives, their kids, their mother, their iwi.

But the songs coming out of radios then could also seem absurdly at odds with the world into which they were being cast. This was illustrated with perfect Tarantino-esque irony when John Hanlon's breezy 1974 single 'Lovely Lady' played over the closing credits of *How To Murder Your Wife*, the 2015 teledrama on the true story of suburban wife-killer Alfred Benning.

The musicians I saw at the Union Hall had been predominantly male. There was the rare exception. Baby, Ragnarok and 1953 Memorial Society Rock 'n' Roll Band all had a female singer, in each case the lone woman in the line-up. For a brief time Mammal featured Julie Needham on vocals and violin. But there is no question that rock was a masculine world. Even with *The Little Red Schoolbook* to guide me, and a mother who read Germaine Greer, I hardly stopped to question the male hegemony of the music scene.

By the end of the decade punk had arrived and put paid to all that. Punk started from the idea that anyone could be in a band: three chords and you were away. In many ways it restored the old idea of pop as entertainment, something that had been lost in the earnest musicality of '70s rock. Women now claimed a place on the stage, and it didn't matter that they hadn't spent the previous decade woodshedding their Eric Clapton guitar licks. The way The Wide Mouthed Frogs charmed and commanded the crowds proved that.

During the decade New Zealand had seen cultural changes far beyond musical ones. In 1972, after twelve years of National rule, the country had elected a Labour government. The new prime minister, Norman Kirk, had revived a sense of social justice and moral responsibility that had seemed desperately compromised under Keith Holyoake, whom poet James K. Baxter had dubbed Mr Mouldybroke. Kirk was not a member of the counterculture. In many ways his views were conservative. He opposed abortion and homosexual law reform, for example. Yet under him New Zealand felt like a place where a discussion of dreams might at least be possible. He withdrew New Zealand troops from Vietnam, joined an international boycott on sporting relations with South Africa, and barred visits by nuclear warships. He even sent a New Zealand naval frigate, with a member of parliament on board, into the Pacific to protest against French nuclear testing at Mururoa.

Kirk's sudden death after less than two years in office, followed by the 1975 victory of National's Robert Muldoon, altered the mood. If the counterculture had enjoyed a moment of optimism under Kirk, it quickly became embattled under Muldoon. A pugnacious man with a bad temper and a malevolent grin, Muldoon took an aggressive stance towards anyone who might not agree with him. He despised academics. He decried 'trendy lefties'. He once hit a protester outside a meeting of the Landlords Association, where he had given a speech and stayed on for a few drinks. He often talked about 'the ordinary bloke', a notional person on whose behalf he was fighting. The ordinary bloke seemed to be a New Zealand male who just wanted to be able to do a day's work, go home, drink beer and watch rugby. Anyone with progressive views on education, environment or equality was the prime minister's natural enemy.

A distinguished music professor once told me what happened when he was introduced to Muldoon at a function. As he began to explain the nature of his work, the country's leader snorted, 'Classical music? Huh. I don't have time for *that*.'

Muldoon didn't have much time for pop music either. He resisted a lobby that wanted to lift the forty percent sales tax on records, although he maintained the exemption for soft-porn magazines such as *Penthouse* and *Playboy*. From the middle of the

'70s the number of local recordings went into a marked decline, with record companies unable to justify the investment in a small market.

In 1980 the New Zealand band Mi-Sex, riding high on having had an Australian hit with their song 'Computer Games', invited Muldoon to attend their concert at Wellington Town Hall and witness pop music as a viable form of cultural expression. He accepted the invitation, appeared to enjoy himself, and didn't use the earplugs provided. But he still didn't drop the sales tax.

In spite of a national conservatism embodied by Muldoon, middle New Zealand, the people the prime minister liked to refer to as 'Rob's Mob', gradually began to adopt some of the trappings of the counterculture. Rugby players grew their hair – at least long enough to cover their collars and cauliflower ears. Policemen sprouted sideburns and moustaches. Even marijuana was no longer solely the vice of anti-authoritarian longhairs.

Pissheads were starting to smoke pot, while farmers – diehard National voters – had begun to dabble in crop diversification of an illegal kind.

In music, too, ideas that had once seemed outlandish had to some extent infiltrated the broadcast frequencies. Shortly before Blerta disbanded in 1976, they were given their own series of television programmes. Like the success of Space Waltz's 'Out on the Street' a year earlier, the Blerta series showed how the symbols of rebellion and dissent could be assimilated and accepted, particularly if they were presented in the same safe packages as other entertainment.

But if middle New Zealand co-opted a few bohemian trappings, unrest continued to blossom on both sides of the divide. Rising oil prices and loss of unrestricted access to the British market, both forces beyond Muldoon's control, brought a steep rise in unemployment and a drop in real income. Māori and Pacific Islanders were hit particularly hard. In an effort to keep things the way they were, Muldoon increased subsidies to farmers and instigated such grand schemes as construction of the Clutha Dam, which involved flooding a beautiful valley and got him offside with the burgeoning environmental movement. Meanwhile the alcohol industry went from strength to strength. The desire of New Zealanders to numb their minds appeared to be on the rise. The breweries were there to provide the means and profit from it. Sometimes it felt as though the country was divided between those who thought the answer was to get rid of Muldoon and those who thought it was just to play more rugby and drink more beer.

25
ON THE STREET

The 1980s arrived and I was a newly unemployed musician in a city suddenly brimful of bands. Wellington seemed to be fizzing with dangerous energy. Punk had kicked open the imaginations of a lot of people who had not previously thought of themselves as musical. Everybody's flatmate seemed to be wielding an instrument. The best of them made up for lack of expertise with attitude and energy.

I would go to parties and find a band mid-performance in a living room, amplifiers propped up on armchairs, and to suburban halls, where groups were mounting their own shows. The more accomplished of the new breed sometimes played at the Rock Theatre. A lot of these bands, among them The Wallsockets, Naked Spots Dance and Life in the Fridge Exists, lived in flats near the university. The members had the air of academic refugees, and the crowds they attracted were a mix of similarly disaffected intellectuals, anarchist mischief-makers and bootboys looking for trouble.

At a flat on The Terrace I found myself in an impromptu

jam with a left-handed guitarist called Kevin Hawkins. I'd seen his group Shoes This High at Rock Theatre. Their angular and intense music reminded me a little of the Captain Beefheart records I'd listened to back at Onslow and I liked Kevin's playing. Our jam session, though, was doomed. As Kevin wrestled some animal howls from his instrument and I tried to find a bass part that might fit, he seemed stoned and distracted. The painter Tony Fomison was having an argument with his brother in the corridor outside and the session was soon abandoned.

Around the same time, my North Terrace household was visited by two brothers, Dan and Nino Birch, decadent dandies who had grown up in Hong Kong and acted as though they had seen something the rest of us hadn't and were going to show us provincials a thing or two. They would stand in our front room and, in their posh accents, make such pronouncements as: 'There have never been any good bands in New Zealand.' They meant to remedy this, and formed a trio called Beat Rhythm Fashion. The name reflected the loftiness of their demeanour, as though they could not play pop music without passing a comment on its simplicity and disposability. They weren't strong singers but their tunes were weirdly haunting and their lyrics mourned a society they saw as suffocating on its own complacency. The music was persuasive, even if its creators were obnoxious.

More fun was a band of Onslow College students I caught one night on a five-band bill at Thistle Hall. They called themselves The Rodents, which was apt as the stage seemed to be infested with them. I couldn't count how many there were, as none stood still long enough. They had several guitarists, a couple of saxophone players, singers, a keyboardist and at least three drummers, although only a single drum kit. One of them would command this while the others hovered like reserves, ready to take the sticks should their bandmate show signs of fatigue, which sometimes occurred mid-song. They played everything at a rapid tempo, and I recognised many of their songs as sped-up versions of the Rough Justice repertoire. It turned out they had been regulars at Last Resort and had studied us closely.

While some of the new bands intrigued me I couldn't imagine joining any of them, and before long I was making music with Bill Lake again. If punk had left any impression on Bill, it was only to convince him there might be hope after all for a band as ramshackle as the Strugglers. He had begun writing songs with Arthur Baysting and we learned a few of them in the basement flat of the Strugglers' drummer, Steve Hunt. Bill, Steve, Andrew Delahunty and I began to perform occasionally, sometimes as the Strugglers, sometimes as The Ducks.

Bill had no ambition to make music his profession. He was working as a postie at the Central Post Office and mentioned there might be a job going there. I signed up the following Monday. Like making music, walking around Wellington was something I'd loved to do long before I'd thought about doing it for a living. From the time I could walk, my dad had taken me for what he called 'rambles and scrambles'. He'd put his pipe in his pocket, a few provisions in a pack, and we'd head off for an afternoon in Bolton Street Cemetery, or up the hills above Khandallah where he'd played as a child. A few years later my brother Tim and I began rambling and scrambling on our own. On winter days when Tinakori Hill was covered in mist we would put on our coats and climb the track from the top of Thorndon's

St Mary Street in search of the cave where we'd heard a hermit lived. Other times we'd jump the fence at the Highbury end of the reservoir and bushwhack our way down to the dam, trying to avoid the park rangers, or roam the no man's land behind the office buildings on The Terrace, where we'd find such treasures as old letter blocks discarded by nearby printing factories.

Now, as a postie, I got to know the city even more intimately, learning the backyard shortcuts, the bush tracks and switchbacks, and how to dodge the dogs. The route I was assigned took me high above the city, where I could look down at the tops of the buildings surrounding the harbour and see homes clinging to the hills. I'd never stop for long: the harder the rain and colder the wind, the faster I moved and the sooner my working day was over.

The hours were not very rock 'n' roll – seven a.m. starts, six days a week. Yet in some ways the post office resembled a bigger version of the Rough Justice bus. There were about forty posties at the central branch: actors, poets, musicians, gardeners, linguists, philosophers, communists, gamblers and junkies, all glad to have found a job that paid them enough to live on and left enough hours in the day to live their other lives. Posties talked to each other while they sorted their mail (and one or two talked to themselves). We would discuss music, movies, books and the excellence of the date scones at the government-subsidised cafeteria on the next floor, but you couldn't let the conversation slow you down. When, at nine o'clock, the supervisor called, 'Clear down!' you had to be ready to bundle your letters, throw them in your canvas bag and get out the door.

Some posties lasted only a short while. I sensed the career of one new recruit would be brief when I spied him, from the other side of the cafeteria, making his way painstakingly from the tea urn to the table where the rest of us were sitting, a full cup of tea balanced on top of his head. I never found out whether he spilt any – by the time he would have reached the table the rest of us were back downstairs sorting our mail. When I returned that afternoon after completing my round, I was not surprised to see him still busy at the sorting case. It would be nightfall by the time his customers received their mail.

Other posties had worked there for years. Tall Malcolm knew every walk in Wellington and could get around his deliveries faster than anyone. When I began he had already been a postie for a decade. He spoke half a dozen languages, and would store up his leave and take off to Rajasthan or Mongolia before reappearing a few months later, the same stooping, sandalled, straggly-haired streak of lightning.

By early 1981 the sorting-case conversation had turned to the coming visit of the Springbok rugby team from South Africa. When Norman Kirk had become prime minister in 1972, he had called off a Springbok tour, knowing this would make him unpopular with the rugby and beer brigade but concerned about likely violence and the way the country would be viewed on the world stage. 'When it comes to a decision between what I must do in the light of the facts that are put before me ... and a desire to avoid criticism, then I would be failing in my duty if I did not accept the criticism and do what I believed to be right,' he had said. Nine years later Muldoon, who referred to anti-tour organisations such as HART (Halt All Racist Tours) and CARE (Citizens Association For Racial Equality) as 'traitors', told the New Zealand Rugby Football Union that if they wanted to host a South African rugby tour it was up to them.

On July 17, 1981 the Springboks arrived.

Earlier in the year I'd gone to a weekend session in the Union Hall, where HART organisers had briefed us on strategies they would use to stop the games should the tour go ahead. We had divided into groups, linked arms and practised ways of resisting the police. I'd been going on protest marches since I was a kid but this was new. In the past it had been a matter of showing up, grabbing a banner and joining the crowd for a stroll on the street. This seemed much more serious.

Not long before the tour began, Boyd told me a weird story. He had been driving home to Plimmerton one night after a gig in town when he passed a house where police had been called to a rowdy party. What he saw through his windscreen wasn't the usual cop car, couple of constables and a noise control officer. A phalanx of uniformed men in full riot gear of helmets, visors and batons were rounding up what looked like a typical bunch of Saturday night revellers. It had reminded him of a scene from Roger Donaldson's 1977 dystopian film *Sleeping Dogs*.

We would later learn that the police had created two special squads – Red and Blue – and sent them to Hawai'i for training. At its team-building sessions the Red Squad had developed its own motivational chant: 'Root more, eat more, drink more piss! Red, Red, Red's the best!' Had what Boyd witnessed been a dress rehearsal?

At work I argued with a postie who said politics should stay out of sport. Other posties got involved in the protests. Some took roles as marshals and organisers. Once the two-month tour kicked off there was a march in Wellington every Wednesday and Saturday, the days on which the games were taking place in different parts of the country. I joined half of them. In Hamilton, the second match of the tour was cancelled after hundreds of protesters cut their way through a fence and stormed the field.

The police, caught by surprise, were helpless to stop them. Although they eventually arrested many of the protesters, they were also forced to shield them from the wrath of enraged rugby-goers.

In Wellington the following Wednesday, a peaceful evening march on Molesworth Street was set upon by baton-wielding cops, leaving people in the front lines bloodied and wounded. It felt like revenge by the police for their humiliation in Hamilton. From then on, like many others I would dress in a motorcycle helmet and stuff newspapers under my clothing. The chant 'Remember Soweto!' became 'Remember Molesworth Street!'

The protests were planned like a military campaign. On the day of the Wellington test match we were marshalled into groups. Those prepared to brave a possible baton charge were ushered into one squad and given special instructions. The group of several hundred that I joined was designed as a decoy to confuse the cops and stretch their resources. We formed a rambling stop–start procession around the winding roads above Athletic Park, where the game was to take place. We passed throngs of rugby fans heading to the game and dodged the odd bottle, beer can and 'Fuck you!' hurled in our direction. We didn't know what was happening elsewhere. Later I would read that protesters closer to the game had been bludgeoned by the Red Squad.

Eventually we found ourselves on a field opposite the park. The game was now underway. I could hear the roars of the crowd in the stadium and the chants of protesters in the streets. A line of visored riot police, batons poised and twitching, stood facing us along the perimeter of the field, preventing us getting any closer to the park. As the match went on we held the line

about ten feet away from the police, knowing what would happen if we took a step closer.

As I stood facing down the riot cops, I was no longer thinking about the twenty million or so black South Africans denied a vote, or Nelson Mandela in the nineteenth year of his incarceration for opposing the apartheid regime, or the black activist Steve Biko, tortured and killed by the South African security police. I was thinking about New Zealand, and the strange, violently divided place it seemed to be, a land where people who loved their country were in danger of being killed by other people who, you might say, loved it differently. And I was thinking about my father, and how much of his short life he had devoted to trying to make it a better place, a country built on kindness and imagination, which would give equality to women and men, Māori and Pākehā, workers and bosses, grandparents and children, gays and straights and carnival anarchists. That was the New Zealand that had been dreamed and debated in our living room when I was a kid. Now there was a war going on between that New Zealand and one that seemed to have its origins in some legendary pioneering past, and where our pride as a nation rested on the performance of fifteen men on a rugby field.

That war raged through the whole two months of the tour. There had been a moment after protesters stormed the field in Hamilton when I wondered if Muldoon might intervene and send the Springboks home, but after the battle of Molesworth Street it was clear his intention was to ensure the tour went ahead at any cost.

The final match was at Eden Park in Auckland. That night on TV the area around the park looked like a battlefield. The army had blocked roads with rolls of barbed wire and upturned skip bins. Protesters, dressed for battle with helmets and shields, fought with police in the streets around the grounds. Three protesters dressed as clowns were beaten senseless by members of the Red Squad. The field was flour-bombed from a plane piloted by a man named Marx. In Wellington I sat with hundreds of other protesters blocking a stretch of motorway. We listened to reports from Auckland on a crackly transistor radio. Our rage was tempered by a sense of relief: this would be the last march for now.

26
ANYTHING COULD HAPPEN

The tour found its way into much of the music that came out in its wake. In Wellington, Riot III had formed as a musical and theatrical accompaniment to the Springbok protests, employing the kind of punk iconography that was already a few years out of date. Their singer called himself Void (although we heard his real name was Geoff), wore a fetching combination of leather jacket and kilt, and was an unforgettable presence on the protest marches. The group's single, 'Subversive Radicals', didn't sound as dangerous as it should have. Much more sophisticated was Blam Blam Blam's 'There Is No Depression in New Zealand'. Recorded in July 1981 just as the Springboks were arriving, the song didn't address the subject directly – it had been written before the catastrophic events unfolded – but Richard Von Sturmer's lyric looked back with deep irony on decades of denial.

There is no depression in New Zealand
there are no sheep on our farms,

There is no depression in New Zealand
we can all keep perfectly calm.

Everybody's talking about World War Three.
everybody's talking about World War Three,
But we're as safe as safe can be,
there's no unrest in this country
We have no dole queues,
we have no drug addicts,
we have no racism,
we have no sexism, sexism, no, no

There is no depression in New Zealand
there are no teeth in our heads
There is no depression in New Zealand
we sleep in a well made bed

The Newmatics recorded 'Riot Squad' a month later. This song wasn't really about the tour either – it was inspired by an incident of police brutality at a punk gig – but I could never hear its jaunty reggae without my mind playing images of the Molesworth Street batonings.

Nineteen eighty-one would also see the first release by Herbs, an Auckland group of Māori, Samoan and Pākehā musicians who innovatively combined reggae and Pacific rhythms. Reggae had begun to establish itself in New Zealand from the mid '70s, when the first albums of Bob Marley and The Wailers reached our shores. After Eric Clapton had an international hit with a cover of Marley's 'I Shot the Sheriff', an occasional New

Zealand band could be heard approximating reggae's distinctive offbeat, but only for a song or two. Chaos were the exception. In 1978 Rough Justice had done a few gigs with this pioneering group. Led by a pair of brothers from Porirua, Elmer and Johnny, Chaos played reggae almost exclusively, perhaps the first local band to do so. Yet like so many others they never made a record.

By the time of Bob Marley's visit to New Zealand in 1979, reggae had reached critical mass. Standing at Western Springs that warm afternoon, in a crowd as big as the one Dylan had drawn a year earlier, it became apparent how much this music resonated with New Zealanders in general and Māori in particular. Aston Barrett's basslines pumped deep in my chest as Bob Marley swung his dreadlocks in a trance-like dance and exhorted us to get up, stand up for our rights, while smiling strangers passed me joints.

With its cover depicting the notorious police eviction of Māori protesters from contested land at Auckland's Bastion Point in 1978, Herbs' debut EP *Whats' Be Happen?* offered a local version of some of the ideas Marley had sung about. Phil Toms' song 'One Brotherhood' addressed Māori land rights. 'Azania (Soon Come)', written by Ross France, voiced direct support for the anti-apartheid cause.

But if the tour had a theme tune it was the sombre minor-key melody of Hirini Melbourne's 'Ngā Iwi E'. Thousands of voices could be heard singing it every time we protesters walked the streets, sometimes to the strum of a single guitar, other times a cappella. At the start of one march The Topp Twins led the chorus:

Ngā iwi e! Ngā Iwi e!
Kia kotahi ra te Moana-nui-a-Kiwa
E i a i e
Kia mau ra! Kia mau ra!
Ki te mana motuhake me te aroha
E i a i e
Wahine mā! Wahine mā!
Maranga mai, Maranga mai, kia kaha
E i a i e
Ta ne ma! Ta ne ma!
Whakarongo tautoko kia kaha
E i a i e

All you people! All you people!
Be united as one like the Pacific Ocean
Hold on firmly! Hold on firmly!
To your separate identity and to compassion
All you young women! All you young women!
Rise up, rise up, be strong
All you young men! All you young men!
Listen, support, be strong.

'Ngā Iwi E' was not a song about the tour or the evils of apartheid, but about New Zealand. Bob Marley had sung: *In this great future you can't forget your past*. Hirini Melbourne, too, had been looking to both past and future. Although written and sung in te reo, his song was addressed to Pākehā as well as Māori.

'Ngā Iwi E' called for the people to be 'as one like the Pacific Ocean' yet retain our identities, our links to our ancestors.

For Melbourne this meant his tribal roots in Ngāi Tūhoe and Ngāti Kahungunu. For me it meant remembering my mother and her parents, refugees from Germany, and my father's immigrant ancestors from Germany and Ireland. In entreating young women to rise up and young men to listen and support, the song also celebrated changing gender roles. Women could be leaders; men could be supporters. And to face whatever lay ahead, both needed to be strong.

Eleven weeks after the tour Muldoon won another election. Although his National Party had taken a hit in the main cities, it had surged in rural electorates. He had foreseen this, had known it would be the result of letting the tour go ahead. In the first-past-the-post electoral system he needed only the boost in rural support to win. But for many New Zealanders the tour seemed to have shaken something loose. There was a sense that if a thing was worth doing you'd better get on and do it, even if it meant a fight.

The pubs wouldn't host the punk bands – they were too raw, too young, too dirty – so the bands had organised their own shows in community halls, warehouses and living rooms. Now, post-punk bands were starting to set up their own labels and make their own records. Reggae interpreters Herbs also had their own label, Warrior. In 1981 Blam Blam Blam and Newmatics records came out on Propeller, a small independent label started the year before by Simon Grigg, a young Auckland record store owner. A decade and a half later Grigg would oversee a worldwide hit with OMC's 'How Bizarre'.

In Christchurch, Roger Shepherd, who also worked in a record shop, started Flying Nun Records. The label's second release was a single by a Dunedin trio called The Clean. Formed by brothers Hamish and David Kilgour, The Clean drew on a similar combination of punk and '60s pop as Toy Love, with an extra dose of psychedelia and Dylan. They were raw and their records had a home-made quality, but the choruses stuck like bubblegum and guitarist David Kilgour could coax a thrilling noise from his instrument.

Like Mammal a decade earlier, The Clean had come up with their own idea of cool, but in even greater isolation, without the thought or possibility of making a living but a determination to make music anyway. The spirit was summed up in the chorus of one of their songs: *Anything could happen and it could be right now, the choice is yours to make it worthwhile*. Before their first visit to Wellington a big hand-painted banner appeared in Dixon Street, pasted to the fence around a construction site. It read: 'The Clean Is Coming!' I was reminded of the Blerta posters I'd seen a decade earlier.

One night in the early '80s I was walking home to North Terrace after a movie in town. I'd climbed the Dixon Street steps and was heading up Salamanca Road with the gothic silhouette of Victoria University's Hunter Building looming on my left. Suddenly I was swept back ten years by the sound of an electric guitar at full treble, playing psychedelic scales. With my next steps I could feel the pulse of drums and bass as well. It was Mammal playing in the adjacent Union Hall. No, it wasn't. Mammal were long gone. This was The Clean on the Wellington leg of a campus tour, and as I got closer I could tell the difference. But for a moment, like a Mobius strip, the two ends of a decade had joined and become one.

EPILOGUE

With Muldoon back in government and the pall from the Springbok tour still hanging over New Zealand, I boarded a plane and went to see what the rest of the world looked like. I wasn't sure I wanted to be a musician any more but music was still the fuel that powered my life. I'd spent much of the '70s poring over records from faraway places – London, New York, Memphis, Nashville, New Orleans – trying to figure out what made them sound so good, so unique. I was coming to realise that although music aspired to be universal, it was always the product of a time and place, that a Beatles' single, a Memphis blues, a country ballad or a second-line strut from New Orleans sounded the way it did only because of the lives of the people playing it and the history beneath their feet. Now I wanted to see those places for myself, know what they felt and smelt like, what people ate and drank there, and hear the sounds in the cities that had formed them.

Arriving in America, I was amazed by just how much music there was. There were singers in subways, bands in bars, melodies drifting from parks and balconies. There seemed to be a great appetite for music, and an endless supply.

'So what is your musical preference?' a cab driver with a Creole accent asked me in New Orleans before I'd even mentioned that music was the sole reason for my visit. In that city it felt as though all the sounds of the continent had been washed down the Mississippi River, sloughing off anything unnecessary along the way, bringing only the best. There were brass bands, not the military or Christian ensembles whose plodding dirges I'd heard back home, but carnival combos where sousaphones pumped like the bottom end of a James Brown record. There was a trumpeter playing hymns on Canal Street, holding his instrument with one hand while accompanying himself on an electronic keyboard with the other, and a virtuoso busker in the French Quarter who had built his own drum set out of tins and boxes. Outside my hotel window, a preacher chanted sermons in blues cadences. In a neighbourhood bar I heard men who looked like farmers sawing fiddles and pumping accordions while middle-aged husbands waltzed and two-stepped with their wives. In another, a one-eyed pianist named James Booker seemed to have the entire history of music in his fingertips. He played Chopin and Lead Belly, and all of it sounded like he'd just made it up.

If a song was good and relevant to people's lives, everyone seemed to be playing their version of it. 'Jambalaya (On the Bayou)' had been written in the early 1950s by the Alabama-born country star Hank Williams in celebration of the rich cultural life of the French-speaking Cajuns, who had settled in Louisiana after being driven out of Canada and Maine by the

British. In New Orleans I heard The Neville Brothers perform it as a funk tune, Hackberry Ramblers play it as a two-step, and James Booker make it a manic piano boogie.

The history of the American South is violent and bloody. It is as scarring as that of South Africa's apartheid system, and marked by deeper divisions than those exposed in New Zealand during the Springbok tour. I could feel that history every time someone warned me not to set foot in a particular part of town. I could feel it when I caught the stare of a middle-aged man with the stars and bars emblazoned on his truckers cap, a T-shirt that read 'SONS OF CONFEDERATE VETERANS', and a look on his face that said, 'Have you got a problem with that?' And yet in the music there seemed to be a generosity, and the expression of some kind of collective spirit.

Perhaps I was viewing it all too romantically. After all, many of the musicians seemed to be working for as little pay as any I'd known at home, if not less. I saw amazing musicians who were junkies and derelicts. In New York I went to see a band led by Dannie Richmond, who had been the great drummer for Charles Mingus. I took a seat near the small stage. Dannie wore a tuxedo and looked lean and elegant. With him was a pianist whose brilliant playing could not conceal his tenuous hold on existence. He too wore the semblance of a suit but it was ill-fitting, the cuffs were scuffed, and I was close enough to see that the soles of his shoes were worn through to his socks.

I stayed in Manhattan with some of the musicians who had gone there with Red Mole. Now they had their own band, The Drongos. They were playing most nights but still living hand-to-mouth. When they didn't have a gig they would sometimes busk around Times Square, which had helped them build a following. It occurred to me that in New Zealand musicians of their calibre would never consider playing in the streets. America was tough but the sheer quantity of music, and the way people seemed to take nourishment from it the way they took nourishment from food, was undeniable. I wondered how long it would be before music in New Zealand was as deeply rooted as it seemed to be there, how long before everyone was singing their own version of the same song.

My friends from Rough Justice had flown in other directions. In 1980, following the demise of Rough Justice, Rick Bryant had moved to Auckland and joined a punchy five-piece band called Top Scientists, whose original R&B songs had enough in common with Elvis Costello and Graham Parker to have currency in the post-punk world. They played fast and tight and were popular in pubs. Sadly, like most of Rick's bands up to that point, they were never captured on record.

Within a couple of years Rick had teamed up with The Neighbours, a showband led by the irrepressible Sam Ford, with Trudi Green as one of the three lead singers. On the side he started an eleven-piece soul band called The Jive Bombers, which eventually became his most successful musical enterprise. It didn't hurt that the hit movie *The Blues Brothers* had come out in 1980, introducing a new audience to the soul repertoire Rick had always loved to sing, and which Rough Justice had been fruitlessly trooping around the country. At one point The Jive Bombers held the attendance record at the Gluepot. Rick also reunited with Bill Lake, Andrew Delahunty, Geoff Rashbrooke and me in a revived, if very part-time, Windy City Strugglers.

In early 2016 I visited Rick at the central Auckland warehouse that had been his home and rehearsal space for nearly twenty years. I wanted to ask a few questions about the Rough Justice days, to get some dates and facts right. Rick did his best to help but he was more interested in talking about the music he was making now, the gig he had coming up with the Jubilation Choir, and a recording he had been working on with The Jive Bombers. The atmosphere in his home was palpably the same as it had been when I first met him. There were musical instruments, fading band posters, crustacean-encrusted crockery, and thousands and thousands of books. A snaplock bag stuffed with pot sat on the table. But banana boxes and half-cleared shelves signalled changing times: rising rents were forcing him to move west, out of town, away from the community of musicians and urban bohemians by whom he was regarded as a doyen.

As for Graeme Nesbitt, when he had got out of prison in 1978 he found pot had lost its allure but arranging happenings had not. He had been immediately employed by the Wellington City Council to start a programme of summer concerts in the city's parks. This led to a full-time job managing an artists' employment scheme. Several of my old North Terrace flatmates found work through Graeme as painters, performers and puppeteers. He went on to promote events for commercial radio stations. When his brother Rob asked him how he could bring himself to work for people who dispensed such dreadful music, Graeme said one had to remember commercial radio and music were two different things. He also worked as a contract tour manager, overseeing dozens upon dozens of tours, from The Clash to the Chinese Circus.

Life at the higher end of the entertainment business provided Graeme with as much amusement as managing hapless Mammal ever had. A story he was fond of telling concerned the band Talking Heads. In 1984 Graeme had been hired by the promoter of the Sweetwaters South festival in Christchurch to assist the band, but at the hotel Talking Heads' management had brushed him off, saying their American crew would take care of everything. Thus relieved of his duties, Graeme stood back and watched as the musicians and equipment were loaded on to the bus that would take them to the venue, with the American road manager counting Heads. As the bus drove off Graeme ducked into an adjacent tobacconist's to buy a newspaper, where he was approached by David Byrne, Talking Heads' leader, who asked in bewilderment, 'Have you seen my band?'

Graeme's tour-managing skills extended to non-performing celebrities. He managed the visit of Pope John Paul II in 1986, and shepherded a party of rugby supporters on an All Blacks tour of Australia. He also found a new addiction: running. Every Sunday he would jog the thirty kilometres from his flat in Northland to his parents' home in Upper Hutt to join the family for roast dinner. He would clock up a hundred kilometres a week. With a group of former inmates he started a team. They named it The Drug Runners.

In the 1990s he went to live in Malaysia. Some of his friends said it was to get away from alcohol, on which he was becoming increasingly dependent. Based in Kuala Lumpur, he sobered up, resumed his academic career and taught English. He converted to Islam and married a presenter for Malaysia state television.

The last time Rick spoke to his old mate was on the phone in

2000. Graeme had been diagnosed with cancer. They reminisced about high times and fallen comrades but Graeme soon sounded tired.

'I don't know what to say,' Rick admitted.

'Why don't you sing to me?' Graeme said.

Rick sang him a blues. Graeme died a month later, in June 2000. He was forty-nine.

Around the time Graeme Nesbitt was released from jail, Richard Holden was promoted from Lion Breweries' entertainment manager to be head of its export division, which more or less marked the end of his involvement with New Zealand music. Other events, however, kept growing. He waged a campaign to launch Steinlager on the international market, turning Lion's export division into a multimillion-dollar enterprise. Then he went to work for Australian rival Foster's, insinuating the Aussie brand into the New Zealand market with sponsorship of such grand occasions as the Wellington Cup at Trentham Racecourse. The bacchanalian hospitality of his sponsor's tent was legendary.

He ran polo tournaments, hired fleets of helicopters, drove the latest Jaguars, commissioned specially bred roses, and became a designer of women's frocks, winning Melbourne Cup raceday fashion contests several years in a row. He got the nickname Golden Holden. In 1998 he ran unsuccessfully for the Auckland mayoralty. He died in 2008, yet even at his funeral he continued to entertain, blowing kisses from a giant screen and thanking everyone for coming.

And what became of the pub circuit he had created? In late 2014 I visited the offices of Lion Breweries in South Auckland to see if any records remained from the days when there were 300 musicians on the company payroll and Richard Holden was managing an annual entertainment budget of several million dollars. The company's librarian, Edna Carson, was helpful but there was little on paper from Holden's era. It seemed many files had been destroyed when the head office moved from Wellington to Auckland in the '80s.

After Holden, Lion effectively gave up organising big tours by high-profile bands and left music promotion to the independents, who often used Lion pubs as venues. There continued to be a demand for entertainment in provincial taverns, but economics made small units preferred. In what remained of the Lion files I found press releases for dozens of imported entertainers, usually duos or soloists, contracted by Lion in the early '80s. The record was dismal. 'Entertainer Tony Bee will do anything for a laugh,' read one press release. 'Some nights the forty-two-year-old singer-comedian might put on a wig and rabbit ears and play "Bright Eyes". Tony, currently touring Lion Breweries pubs, has been pulling these sorts of stunts for about ten years, when he left his job as a steward with the British merchant navy...'

Another reported: 'Peter Morley had had enough of singing and playing the guitar by 1973 but now he's back in the business and touring New Zealand, all because of an incident in a Welsh nightclub.' And then there was this: 'Scottish guitarist Buddy Martin came out of musical retirement to visit New Zealand for the first time. The opportunity of playing the pub circuit made him drop his business for a while and pick up his guitar again. He already admits he has fallen in love with New Zealand. The scenery is amazing and the people friendly.'

Thinking about the campus underground and the pub circuit – the parallel empires Graeme Nesbitt and Richard Holden once presided over – I find myself comparing the two men. Nesbitt was not acquisitive. Other than a few books or musical instruments he appeared to have no interest in material things. Nor did he hold on to money: anything he made went straight into funding the next freak out. Holden led an opulent life with a three-storey Ponsonby villa, expensive cars and impeccably tailored suits. Yet in spite of their contrasting agendas, the two men seemed possessed by similar drives. Both were furiously energetic. Both were compelled to create the big event. And both died young, Nesbitt at forty-nine, Holden at sixty.

There were only two and a half years between them in age. They grew up in the same place, Trentham in the Hutt Valley, although Holden had been sent away to live with his father on Motuihe Island a few years before the Nesbitts arrived from the Hokianga. Did they ever meet? No one I've spoken to can recall such an occasion. Yet in a country the size of New Zealand it is hard to imagine they didn't.

I picture a scene. It is a late summer afternoon in the early 1970s. Sunlight is streaming through the windows of the Spectrum Bar, causing a smell of warm beer to rise from the carpet, which is still sticky from the venue's christening the night before, at which Prime Minister Holyoake was in attendance. Graeme Nesbitt looks down at the loud purple and orange swirls and imagines what the patterns might do if he was tripping. A broad balding man in a pastel blue suit and bright red shirt with a huge pointed collar strides across the room towards him, a flute glass of champagne in each of his meaty hands. He proffers a glass to his longhaired guest, who is surveying the stage, the PA stack and the lighting rig.

'So how many does the room hold?' Nesbitt asks.

'Well we could fit 300 of your hippies in here, no problem,' Richard Holden says. 'But what's the point if they're only going to drink orange juice?'

'If you put LSD in the orange juice you could sell it for more than your godawful piss,' Nesbitt says.

They chuckle. 'It's a deal,' says the man in the suit, but they know it isn't. 'You know, I won't be in this pub game forever. Beer and bands, bands and beer. I've got other plans. Racehorses. Department stores. Frock designs. The mayoralty perhaps? I'm serious. What about you? There has to be more to life than babysitting varsity stoners.'

'Sure, there are some big acts I'd like to tour. The Pope. I'm not joking. And I'm going to make Dragon the biggest band in Australasia. But look, I must be off. I've got a car boot full of buddha sticks to shift before I can pay Split Ends for tonight's show up the hill.'

'And I've got Frankie Stevens doing the floor show here with the Quincys, and all this godawful piss to sell.'

And what of the others? Peter Kennedy, Mike Gubb, Tony Backhouse and my schoolfriends Stephen Jessup, Martin Highland and Boyd have all continued to devote themselves to music of various kinds, in various parts of the world. But of all the people I encountered during my time with Rough Justice, the one I had wondered about most was Janet Clouston. After finishing art school in Auckland, she had moved to Australia. I wasn't sure how she felt about her days with Rough Justice. The way I remembered it, she had always been working at least as hard as any of the musicians on stage, with little credit or reward.

When I skyped her, Janet agreed this was probably the case, and seemed happy to hear it acknowledged, yet she recalled the days of the bus with laughter and affection. She reminded me of things I'd forgotten, such as an incident at a Greymouth motor camp. We had arrived under cover of darkness and the proprietor had seemed friendly enough as he gave us the keys to our cabins. But when the sun rose next morning to reveal the bus in all its painted glory he became irrational. Accusing us of harbouring stowaways, he ordered us off the property, but before we could leave he parked a trailerload of pig's swill across the path of the bus, shouting, 'It's too late, I've called the police!' The police had evidently had dealings with the hysterical motelier before. When they arrived they gently insisted he move the trailer.

During our conversation I wondered out loud what had finally happened to the bus.

'I sold it,' Janet said.

I was surprised. '*You* sold it? But the bus was Rick's, wasn't it?

'No, of course not,' she laughed. 'Rick never had any money. The bus was mine.'

KOENIG

Coda: 'Freedom St Marys'

In 2015, after living in Auckland for nearly ten years, I returned to Wellington with a need to retrace the paths I'd trodden at different times in my life. I had felt this compulsion before after shorter absences but never so strongly. I went looking for the shortcuts I remembered from my postie days. I climbed the zigzag to the Thorndon house where Rough Justice used to rehearse, and I retraced the journey from my first flat to our family home in North Terrace, the route I had taken on the morning my father died.

Tonight I've climbed the hill to Kelburn the way I used to on a Friday night in my early teens, when I was giddy with music after seeing bands at the Union Hall. Sometimes I'd stop by the old Skyline Tearooms at the top of the Cable Car, look down at the lights of the city and the black hole of the harbour, and hear the last band still playing in the distance. Tonight the wind has caught a handful of remembered beats and is blowing them in my direction. It's Bruno. He's drumming wildly, like the time I saw him splinter his sticks and smash his cymbals to the floor, with every beat still somehow falling in the perfect place. I recognise the song, 'Freedom St Marys'. It's the song that told me, more than any other, what this crazy music I was in love with was trying to do.

Nobody ever told you it was going to be easy.

Bruno was in his thirties. He had been a professional musician for more than a decade – in Australia with high-flying bands such as Max Merritt and The Meteors, in New Zealand with The Quincy Conserve, and wherever he could playing jazz – when he started Blerta with his brother-in-law Geoff Murphy, who played the trumpet. The rest of Blerta were younger, mostly refugees from the rock world. Jazz people often sniffed at rock, dismissed it as kids' stuff, but to Bruno it offered the freedom jazz was supposed to have: from the predictable cabaret routines, the pub circuit, the cheesy collar-and-tie gigs.

For Blerta, life was an improvisation. They would turn up in a town unannounced in their Day-Glo-spattered bus and look for somewhere to play, somewhere to stay. They were making it up as they went along. Nobody told anyone what to do or not do.

Nobody ever told you, that's the name of the game.

'Freedom St Marys' was Blerta's manifesto. It was my favourite song of their live shows, the part where the band went into overdrive, but it is also the best record they ever made. Bruno had composed the song with the band's brilliant young piano player, Chris Seresin. The body of the tune is a riff by Seresin, a repetitive series of two-note phrases played on an electric keyboard hooked up to a wah-wah pedal. The riff tumbles like a moving carriage along the high-speed railway line of Bruno's drumming.

To run with the wind and laugh with the sea, begins the second verse. It is a line of its time, the kind an author in a tie-dyed T-shirt might have written in a children's book in 1972, the year the song was released, yet when Corben Simpson sings the words they rage. He pushes his voice higher and higher, beyond its natural limits. He gets even more strident in the next section, where Bruno's lyrics confront the real situation. *Born in freedom, dressed in chains, everybody loses, nobody gains.* Kemp Tuirirangi's guitar answers every phrase, making its own wild bid for freedom, but more than anything it is Bruno's drumming that embodies the lyric. He explodes time. He halves the beat, then gleefully doubles it. He plays like an escaped convict who will never be caught. He has cast off the last chains of conformity. He is truly free, and daring the rest of the band to follow him.

Nobody ever told you it was going to be easy.

By the time I finished school Blerta was over. Geoff Murphy was to become a pioneer of New Zealand cinema, and Bruno would find his new métier as an actor in films such as Murphy's *Utu* and *The Quiet Earth* and Roger Donaldson's *Smash Palace*, and in an Australian television series, *Frontline*. His timing on screen was as natural and precise as it was behind the drums. He portrayed a surprising range of characters, yet for each he drew on some deep core of Bruno-ness. There was the widower Williamson in *Utu*, driven mad by grief; the scientist Zac Hobson in *The Quiet Earth*, alone in a world suddenly emptied of human life; Al Shaw in *Smash Palace*, a father turned fugitive. Each man was trapped by a terrible set of circumstances yet somehow found his way free, either through madness or imagination. Bruno's performances drew on what he understood freedom to be.

The only rules he trusted and lived by were his own.

Although he kept playing drums in brief stints with pop bands such as The Crocodiles and occasional jazz gigs, Bruno seemed just as creative and happy in his new career. He died of cancer in June 1995. He had been taken ill while on an Australian film shoot in January and had returned to New Zealand. His tangi took place at Taupunga Marae, just up the road from Snoring Waters, the piece of land in the tiny Hawke's Bay town of Waimārama that members of the Blerta clan had bought communally in the '70s. Most of the clan had since moved away, leaving just Bruno, his wife Veronica, any number of their five children, and the occasional grandchild. I drove up for the tangi with Bill Lake, who had known Bruno since the days of Mammal. Like a Blerta gig it was unorthodox, a mix of Māori, Pākehā, Ratana, Catholic and probably pagan rituals, presided over by Ronnie Smith, a jazz musician whom Bruno had played with in the 1960s and who was now a Ratana priest.

As the numbers grew it became apparent just how many people loved Bruno, and how varied they were. As New Zealand's Hollywood star Sam Neill read a tribute from Australia-based comedian John Clarke, a mourner was pointed out to me as a reformed safe-cracker, 'a very good one'. Rick Bryant was there. As the sun went down I saw him with Ian Watkin heading away from the crowds, towards the middle of a paddock. Soon the only thing visible in the darkness was the glowing end of a smoldering object passing back and forth between them.

I recognised Corben Simpson, standing beside a battered vehicle that seemed to be his home, changing from one crumpled shirt into another. Someone said he was recently out of jail. Chris

Seresin looked stricken, as though he had tried to run with the wind but the wind had turned around and kicked him in the teeth.

Freedom had been the catchcry of the counterculture, shouted in the '60s and echoing into the '70s and beyond. It was the slogan of the civil rights and anti-apartheid movements, the war protesters, the pro-cannabis campaigners, and Bill Dwyer's carnival anarchists. But the pursuit of freedom had proved to be dangerous. For some it had led to imprisonment. Others had felt the blows of police batons. A few were dead or damaged by drugs. At Bruno's tangi it seemed almost as if that idea of freedom – and all the idealism it embodied – had finally found its resting place.

But in a performance, a recording, or even the remembering of a piece of music, dreams stay alive. This is what I am thinking as I stand on the Kelburn skyline hearing Bruno drumming 'Freedom St Marys', although the only sound is the clatter of the Cable Car going over a bridge.

Acknowledgements

The original manuscript of this book was written in 2015 as a thesis for the MA in Creative Writing at the International Institute of Modern Letters, Victoria University of Wellington. It has benefitted greatly from the feedback of my fellow students: Jane Arthur, Louise Compagnone, Alexandra Hollis, Helen Hunter, Sam Lentle-Keenan, Nina Powles, Simon Thomas, Sarah Webster and Louise Wrightson, not to mention the creative guidance of our supervisor Cliff Fell. I am also grateful to Tom McWilliams and Fergus Barrowman, who along with Cliff were my assessors and made valuable recommendations.

Thanks to Chris Price and Harry Ricketts for encouraging me to do the MA in the first place; Paul Amies, Arthur Baysting, Chris Bourke, Stephen Canning, Mark Derby, Kathy McRae and Nic Smith, all of whom gave many useful notes; Redmer Yska for countless illuminating conversations; Matthew McKee and Keith Stewart for trawling their photographic archives; Peter Dasent and Andrew Delahunty for fact-finding and field work; Creative New Zealand for a grant to conduct interviews towards this project; Edna Carson for helping me navigate the library of New Zealand Breweries; the staff of the National Library of New Zealand and the libraries of Auckland University and Victoria University of Wellington; Infofind – Radio New Zealand Reference Library; Mary Varnham, Emma Wolff and

Sarah Bennett at Awa Press, Jane Parkin, and Denis and Verna Adam and the Adam Foundation.

Thanks to everyone who spoke, corresponded or shared stories or helped in other ways: Susan Belt, Thomasin Bollinger, Tim Bollinger, Clinton Brown, Rod Bryant, Janet Clouston, Mike Corless, Paul Davies, John Dix, Bernadine Doyle, Tim Finn, Peter Frater, Ray Goodwin, Charley Gray, Jackie Matthews, Tina Matthews, Jan Melbourne, Mahina Melbourne, Rob Nesbitt, Robert Nesbitt Snr., Nigel Poysden, Chris Prowse, Trevor Reekie, Alastair Riddell, Chris Seresin, Rachel Stace, Jim Stevenson, Robert Taylor, Richard Von Sturmer and Sally Zwartz.

Special thanks to Rick Bryant and all the former members and crew of Rough Justice: Tony Backhouse, Janet Clouston, Mike Gubb, Martin Highland, Stephen Jessup, Peter Kennedy, Dennis Mason, Simon Page, Malcolm Prendevile, and Boyd.

The author and publisher are grateful for permission to quote extracts from the following lyrics: 'Play Nasty For Me' lyrics by Tony Backhouse; 'Sunshine' lyrics by Paul Hewson, © EMI Music Publishing Australia Pty Limited; 'The Hills Are Alive…' lyrics by The Wide Mouthed Frogs; 'There Is No Depression In New Zealand' lyrics by Richard Von Sturmer ; 'Nga Iwi E' written by Hirini Melbourne; 'Freedom St Marys' written by David Lawrence and Chris Seresin, © EMI Music Publishing Australia Pty Limited

Selected discography

I have included only records by New Zealand artists here; there are other places you can go to find out about the best of B.B. King, James Brown, The Beatles or Van Morrison. I have not tried to be exhaustive, but rather noted a few favourites by each act while hoping to give an idea of the breadth of their work. In some cases I refer to private, unreleased or deleted recordings. This is not to deliberately frustrate you, but to give these lost recordings the status they deserve – and perhaps hasten the day they are made widely available. Many of the individual tracks mentioned can be found on Spotify and YouTube.

BILLY TK AND THE POWERHOUSE

Move On Up: The Unreleased 1972 HMV Tapes (EMI CD, 2009)

Life Beyond the Material Sky (Little Wing album, 1990)

After leaving Human Instinct in 1971, Billy Te Kahika formed The Powerhouse, a fluid ensemble of anything up to 15 members. *Move On Up: The Unreleased 1972 HMV Tapes* captures the band in its embryonic phase, covering Curtis Mayfield, Van Morrison and Neil Young. Over the next few years Te Kahika would become increasingly influenced by the jazz–rock fusion of Carlos Santana and John McLaughlin. This period is represented by *Life Beyond the Material Sky*, a live 1975 recording from Wellington's St James Theatre released by German label Little Wing.

BLAM BLAM BLAM

'There Is No Depression in New Zealand'/'Got to Be Guilty' (Propeller single, 1981)

Maids To Order (Propeller EP, 1981)

Luxury Length (Propeller album, 1982)
The Complete Blam Blam Blam (Festival/Mushroom CD, 2003)

No single track captures more vividly the uneasy mood of the country in 1981 than Blam Blam Blam's 'There Is No Depression in New Zealand', although similar strains of paranoia and division run through many other Blams' songs, including 'Blue Belmonts' from the *Maids To Order* EP ('the Secret Service makes us nervous') and 'Got to Be Guilty', about the scapegoating of the wrongfully convicted Arthur Allan Thomas. By the time the Blams released their only studio album, their sound had grown more sophisticated, without giving up its edge. Tim Mahon's spiky basslines sound as though they are being played on an instrument strung with barbed wire. 'Don't Fight It Marsha, It's Bigger Than Both of Us' turns to personal politics and hints at the career Don McGlashan would go on to have as one of the country's most beloved singer-songwriters. All the material mentioned can be found on the 2003 compilation *The Complete Blam Blam Blam*.

BLERTA
'Freedom St Marys' (HMV single, 1972)
'Aunty Ada' (HMV single, 1972)
'This Is the Life' (HMV single, 1974)
The Return Trip (EMI CD, 2001)

When an Australian interviewer asked Blerta in 1973 if their name meant anything, Bruno Lawrence answered, 'Bruno Lawrence's electric revelations and travelling apparitions'. Pianist Chris Seresin countered with the alternative: 'Bus load of egocentric, raving, tripping adults'. The band could be both. 'Freedom St Marys' was the B-side of Blerta's only hit, 'Dance All Around the World', the Trojan-horse hit that snuck them on to family television as a Golden Disc Awards finalist in 1972, and you'll find a section of this book devoted to it (see pages 247–251) 'Aunty Ada' was the madly uncommercial follow-up: spectacular drumming and a good Seresin keyboard hook, plus an unhinged performance from Simpson of a lyric inspired by a discarded telegram found in a provincial post office. 'This Is the Life' is a bluesy ode to hedonism, written by Geoff Murphy and Ian Watkin. There have been at least three recordings of it, but the best one – if you can find it – is the first. Released only as a single, it features a vocal by Australian singer Renee Geyer, who sings as if she is fully committed to the song's manifesto. Unfortunately, Geyer's contractual conflicts meant the record was quickly withdrawn. *The Return Trip* is a Blerta retrospective compiled by Geoff Murphy, and combines most of the band's singles (although sadly not 'Aunty Ada'), a live 'This Is the Life' (with vocals by Beaver), plus representative selections from Blerta's two albums, *This Is the Life* (1975) and *Wild Man* (1976).

RICK BRYANT

As I have heard Rick Bryant sing on hundreds, perhaps thousands, of occasions, many of his greatest performances exist for me only in memory. On his earliest recordings he is almost unrecognisable as the singer he became. His voice is lighter and less assured, although still capable of conveying deep feeling. There's plenty of that in 'Wild About You', his debut recording with Gutbucket (*In The Blue Vein*, 1969, Ode Records). By the time of the Sam Hunt/Mammal album *Beware The Man* he has grown more confident (see Mammal). But my favourite recordings of Rick are from much later. Some of the performances recorded as Rick Bryant and The Jive Bombers are extraordinary. A standout is 'Time', a wry, sad and soulful memoir, from the album of the same name (Red Rocks, 1999). Since the early '90s Rick has recorded extensively with the reunited Windy City Strugglers. It's hard to be objective. Full disclosure: I produced and played on the recordings. But a few personal favourites are 'Can't Get Back' (*On Top of the World*, 1998), 'Loving You Is Not an Easy Game' (*Kingfisher*, 2005) and 'If I Was Thirsty' (*Shine On*, 2008) – all written by Bill Lake and Arthur Baysting – plus Rick's own tour-de-force 'Snow On the Desert Road' (*Snow on the Desert Road*, 2001).

THE CLEAN

'Tally Ho'/'Platypus' (Flying Nun single, 1981)
Boodle Boodle Boodle (Flying Nun EP, 1981)
Great Sounds Great (Flying Nun EP, 1982)
Anthology (Flying Nun album, 2002)

The Clean introduced their engaging mix of garage-pop, folk-rock and psychedelia with their 1981 debut single 'Tally Ho' and have continued to create fresh music out of those vintage styles, off and on, ever since. The short form suits them best: the early singles and EPs remain their most concise and consistent records. Yet there are fine things to be found throughout their catalogue, a good representation of which can be found on the *Anthology* album.

Interestingly, some four decades after Mammal, Clean guitarist David Kilgour collaborated with Sam Hunt on a pair of albums – *Falling Debris* (Arch Hill, 2008) and *The 8th* (Bandit King, 2015) – that combine Hunt's poetry with Kilgour's blazing guitars.

JOHNNY DEVLIN

'Lawdy Miss Clawdy' (Prestige single, 1958)
How Would Ya Be (Ode CD, 2007)

Already discussed in detail (see pages 127–132) the first version of 'Lawdy Miss Clawdy', if extremely raw, has excitement the remake lacks. It also has the essential spoken intro. *How Would Ya Be*, a bursting-at-the-seams compilation album, contains 37 tracks, all recorded for Phil Warren's Prestige label between 1958 and 1959. Both recordings of 'Lawdy Miss Clawdy' are included, along with such credible slices of south seas rock 'n' roll as Johnny's version of Jimmy Lloyd's 'I Got a Rocket in My Pocket.'

DRAGON

'Education' (Vertigo single, 1975)
Sunshine (CBS album, 1977)
'April Sun in Cuba' (CBS single, 1978)

'I'm Still in Love with You' (CBS single, 1978)

Unlike many bands noted here, Dragon have had a long recording career, from their first albums *Universal Radio* (Vertigo, 1974) and *Scented Gardens for the Blind* (Vertigo, 1975), right up to today. They released EPs of new material in 2011 and 2012, and continue to perform as a live band, led by founder Todd Hunter. Their earliest material is not to my taste: Marc Hunter described it as 'period comedy' and I concur. Nor do I like much of the music they made after the '70s. Their songwriting peak remains *Sunshine*, the first album they made after moving to Australia. Dominated by the songs of Paul Hewson, it captures the ambivalence of a band from provincial New Zealand buzzing on the first rush of international success while navigating the pitfalls of the rock 'n' roll lifestyle that had already cost the life of their first drummer.

'April Sun in Cuba' and 'I'm Still in Love with You' are the best of their Australian hits, both examples of Hewson's genius as a pop craftsman. The first is based on a two-note rock rhumba, mindlessly simple and utterly addictive. The second is a masterpiece of jaded melancholy – remarkable for, among other things, a chorus that simply repeats the verse melody while functioning as the song's central hook. Just before they left New Zealand, the band cut their funkiest single, 'Education'. Robert Taylor sings and plays, while Marc Hunter is relegated to congas. Graeme Nesbitt produces.

HELLO SAILOR

Hello Sailor (Key album, 1977)

Containing the group's three biggest singles – Dave McArtney's 'Gutter Black', Graham Brazier's 'Blue Lady' and Harry Lyon's 'Lyin' in the Sand' – Sailor's debut album represented a milestone in putting original indigenous songs before a receptive local audience. Elsewhere on their first and finest album are further snapshots of late-night, late '70s Auckland: the loping 'Ponsonby reggae' of 'All Round This Town'; the cautionary tales of 'Hooked' and 'When Your Lights are Out'.

HERBS

Whats' Be Happen? (Warrior EP, 1981)

Light of the Pacific (Warrior album, 1982)

Pacific reggae begins with Herbs' great debut. The six-song *Whats' Be Happen?* doesn't have a bad track, although it's Toni Fonoti's 'Dragons and Demons' and the bilingual title track that stand out, as do Fonoti's songs on the following year's *Light of the Pacific*.

HIGHWAY

Highway (HMV album, 1971)

'This album is for those who want to listen. It was made hurriedly but is an honest effort,' begin the liner notes to the only album these Wellington psych-rock pioneers ever made. Compared to the expansive form that Highway's songs would take on stage, the seven tracks here, averaging seven minutes each, are relatively concise. Singer Bruce Sontgen may not be the most poetic of lyricists, but his gritty vocals provide funky punctuation throughout, while the interplay of guitarists Phil Pritchard and George Barris and the spare groove of bassist George Limbidis and drummer Jim Lawrie remain an exemplar for any band looking for the perfect balance between loose and tight. Favourite tracks are 'Listen to the Band' and 'The Ride' but it's all good.

HUMAN INSTINCT

Burning Up Years (Pye album, 1969)

Stoned Guitar (Pye/Air album, 1970)

Pins In It (Pye album, 1971)

Flamboyant singing drummer Maurice Greer joined veteran Auckland beat group The Four Fours in 1966. Before long they had changed their name to Human Instinct and added Bunnythorpe-born Billy Te Kahika, who brought his Hendrix-influenced guitar skills. Of the three albums made while Te Kahika was with the band, *Stoned*

Guitar is the standout, with the funk-rock evergreen 'Black Sally', two songs by Auckland guitar legend turned Krishna monk Doug Jerebine (also known as Jesse Harper), and the long instrumental title track on which Te Kahika – by now known as Billy TK – sculpts shapes of pure sound from his overdriven Gibson SG guitar.

MAMMAL

Beware the Man, Mammal/Sam Hunt (Red Rat album, 1972)

'Wait'/'Whisper' (Red Rat single, 1973)

'Play Nasty for Me' (unreleased live recording, 1974)

The only album of Mammal ever released is unrepresentative. A collaboration with poet Sam Hunt, it intersperses Hunt's distinctive readings with settings of his poems by Mammal's Tony Backhouse and composer Ian McDonald, and includes interludes by the Alex Lindsay String Quartet and early synthesiser soundscapes. The title song is a powerful piece of psychedelic funk and would remain a staple of the Mammal repertoire. Hunt's lyric, cautioning listeners to '*beware the man who tries to fit you out/in his idea of a hat*' caught the us-against-them mood of the counterculture. Other songs are more pastoral and reflective: 'A Valley Called Moonshine', 'Hot Water Bottle Baby Blues', 'When Morning Comes' and 'A Wind of Wolves' stand out. Mammal's 1973 single paired two originals, 'Wait' and 'Whisper', and gives a greater hint of what this band could be like in full flight. Tony Backhouse's vocal arrangement on Taylor's song 'Wait' is baroque 'n' roll; Backhouse and Bryant's voices are contrasted to great effect on 'Whisper'. But unreleased live recordings (see pages 47–54) come closest to showing what a great and under-documented band this was.

THE MAORI VOLCANICS

Live At The Broderick Inn (Revolution album, 1975)

Although one of the country's longest-running, farthest-travelled showbands, The Maori Volcanics are underrepresented on disc. Nor does the medium really do justice to an act that was comic and visual as much as musical. As it stands, only one side of their 'live' album is in fact live, and intersperses skits of the soon to be legendary Billy T. James (then known as Bill Taitoko) with showy covers of Otis Redding and Joe Tex. The studio side is soul with a Vegas veneer, but Mahora Waaka (later Mahora Peters) shows off her diamond voice on a couple of originals, 'All I Ever Want is You' and 'Mirage'.

THE QUINCY CONSERVE

'Ride the Rain' (HMV single, 1970)

'Everybody Has Their Way' (HMV single, 1970)

Listen to the Band (HMV album, 1970)

Aire of Good Feeling: Best of (EMI CD, 2008)

They released more records than just about any other New Zealand band in the 1970s, but The Quincy Conserve were on disc, as on stage, essentially just a really good covers band, apart from the brief time when Bruno Lawrence was with them. During those few months they cut a number of tracks as good as any of the horn-based rock-jazz bands in the world at the time – think Blood, Sweat & Tears and Chicago. 'Sugar Man' had been a lost single for Bobby Darin, but on the *Listen to the Band* album the Quincys' arrangement improved markedly on the original. Then there were the peerless 'Ride the Rain' (see pages 147–149) and 'Everybody Has Their Way', both Lawrence originals and each philosophical in its own way.

ROCKINGHORSE

'Through the Southern Moonlight' (HMV single, 1975)

Thoroughbred (HMV album, 1975)

Grand Affaire (EMI album, 1976)

Two albums of mellow country-rock. Wayne Mason's song 'Through the Southern Moonlight' (from *Thoroughbred*, but also released as a single) has had a deservedly long life. The south of which it sings might be the American birthplace of country rock, but the song can just as easily be heard as a musical postcard from New Zealand's South Island or, given the swaying palm groove, an island in the South Pacific. Rockinghorse's finest work, though, can be found on the records they made as house band for EMI during this time, backing Māori and Samoan singers such as Mark Williams and The Yandall Sisters. Listen to Williams' 'Sweet Wine' or The Yandalls' 'Sweet Inspiration' for some sweet Pacific soul.

ROUGH JUSTICE

Graeme Nesbitt produced the only commercially released recording of Rough Justice, a song called 'Whitby Success'. Written by Peter Kennedy and Rick Bryant, it appeared on the compilation album *Home Grown* (Radio Windy) in 1979. Four original songs recorded that year when Rough Justice were 2ZM's Band of the Month remain unreleased.

SPACE WALTZ

'Out on the Street' (HMV single, 1974)

Space Waltz (HMV album, 1975)

Alastair Riddell's audacious bid for the glam moment is preserved in Space Waltz's sole long-player. His fondness for early Bowie shows in the occasionally florid lyrics, while elements of his prog past are carried over into the eight-and-a-half-minute 'Seabird'. But if the overall effect is of a slightly overwrought period piece, the high drama of 'Angel' found a surprising fit with the 2014 horror-comedy feature film *Housebound*, where it was a soundtrack highlight.

SHOES THIS HIGH

Shoes This High (STH EP, 1981)

Straight to Hell (Stiltbreeze album, 2014)

The self-titled four-song EP was the only recording Shoes This High released during their brief existence, and always seemed brittle compared to what I heard live. Frontman Brent Hayward, in particular, sounds uncharacteristically subdued. But you can hear the Beefheartisms, especially in 'Not Weighting', where Kevin Hawkins' nervy high-treble guitar rubs and grinds against the other two instrumentalists – bass player Jessica Walker and drummer Chris Plummer – like a bone machine. In 2014, US indie Stiltbreeze released *Straight to Hell*, a full-length album of a live recording from the archive of Bob Sutton, recorded at Billy the Club (formerly Rock Theatre) and capturing this combustible band in all its febrile glory.

SPLIT ENZ

Mental Notes (White Cloud album, 1975)

True Colours (Mushroom album, 1980)

Waiata (Mushroom album, 1981)

Mental Notes was Split Enz's first and arguably greatest album; it's certainly their strangest. Co-writers Phil Judd and Tim Finn probe questions of fear and sanity in unpredictable, disorienting songs, while keyboard player Eddie Rayner burnishes the prog-pop arrangements. While continuing to report from the edge of anxiety, the Enz became increasingly accessible in their following albums, culminating in the pop explosion of *True Colours* and *Waiata*, where Judd's replacement Neil Finn displays his gifts with songs like 'I Got You' and 'One Step Ahead'.

TAMBURLAINE

Say No More (Tartar album, 1972)

The early '70s saw soft rock acts such as James Taylor and Crosby, Stills & Nash serving up antidotes to the nerve-shattering sounds of blues-rock and psychedelia. Tamburlaine produced a local version of the mellow medicine, combining vocal harmonies with intricate acoustic arrangements and a few exceptional songs. Of their two albums, *Say No More* (1972) and *Rebirth* (1973), the former is the stronger. Steve Robinson's Silver Scroll-winning 'Lady Wakes Up', with its 'woodbox of memories', now seems a bit twee, but 'Raven and the Nightingale' rollicks with bluegrass gusto, while 'Pass a Piece of Paper' achieves a perfect balance of melody, harmony and lyrical reflection.

TICKET

Awake (Down Under album, 1971)

Formed in Auckland and hothoused in Christchurch nightclub Aubrey's before an audience of American servicemen on R&R from Vietnam, Ticket were in many ways the epitome of psychedelic blues-rock. Their debut *Awake* is the more exciting of their two albums, showcasing the fluid and deeply Hendrix-inspired guitar of Eddie Hansen and the furiously tight rhythm section of bassist Paul Woolwright and drummer Rick Ball. (Decades later, Woolwright and Ball would play together again with a far more economical style in Hello Sailor.) Frontman Trevor Tombleson's enjoinders to 'free yourself' are very much of their time.

THE TOPP TWINS

Go Vinyl (Dragon's Egg EP, 1982)

Honky Tonk Angel (The Topp Twins album, 2009)

Initially known as yodelling buskers, Huntly-born sisters The Topp Twins became the musical voices of the protest movement, with witty original songs espousing various causes, from nuclear disarmament to gender equity. Hirini Melbourne's 'Ngā Iwi E' was a part of their repertoire as far back as the 1981 Springbok tour, but didn't appear on one of their recordings until the 2009 album *Honky Tonk Angel*, produced by Don McGlashan.

TOY LOVE

'Rebel'/'Squeeze' (Elektra single, 1979)

Toy Love (WEA album, 1980; reissued Real Groovy, 2012)

Live at the Gluepot (Real Groovy album, 2012)

Although Toy Love made an amazing debut single ('Rebel' backed with 'Squeeze') and a couple of follow-ups that were almost as good, their sole self-titled album – produced in Australia by Dragon's Todd Hunter – didn't quite capture the kinetic excitement this band could create on stage. While the songs are almost uniformly great, the sound is spidery and thin. Some of these deficiencies are made up for in the 2012 remastered edition and subsequent *Live at the Gluepot*, recorded on the band's final tour in 1980.

THE WIDE MOUTHED FROGS

Like Rough Justice, the Frogs' only commercial release was on the 1979 *Home Grown* compilation – an early-Motown-style original called 'Someday', co-written with Tony Backhouse.

Sources and notes

PREFACE

'… a decade that New Zealand really experienced in the '70s': Tim Finn, interview with Nick Bollinger for Radio New Zealand, 2014.

MESMERISING ECHOES

Bill Dwyer was born in Ireland and emigrated to New Zealand in 1954. Extroverted and charismatic, he was initially active in the trade union movement in Wellington. In 1960 he founded the Victoria University Anarchist Association. In 1963 he moved to Auckland, where he was prosecuted for neglecting his infant sons, and again for using offensive language while addressing a crowd in Myers Park. By the mid-60s he had moved to Sydney, where he sold thousands of tabs of LSD, was sent to prison and eventually deported. In the United Kingdom he changed his name to Ubique (Latin for 'Everywhere') and launched a festival on a royal hunting ground just south of Windsor. For a few years The Windsor Free Festival brought carnival anarchy to Britain, until Ubique Dwyer was locked up again, this time for creating a public nuisance.

REBELS AND REFUGEES

Denis Glover was a pioneering New Zealand publisher and poet. He wrote satires, lyrics and love poems but is most fondly remembered for 'The Magpies', New Zealand's most widely anthologised poem.

James K. Baxter was one of New Zealand's best-loved poets. His first collection was published in 1944, when he was eighteen. A stern social critic and champion of the disenfranchised, in the late 1960s he founded a commune in the tiny riverside community of Jerusalem near Whanganui, where he took on the bearded and barefooted manner of a biblical prophet.

Colin McCahon is credited with introducing modernism to New Zealand painting, and is regarded as the country's most significant modern artist.

Douglas Lilburn was one of New Zealand's most admired classical composers, combining European training and a distinctively New Zealand voice.

'YOU CAN'T DRESS LIKE THAT IN THE HUTT'

'All Along the Watchtower', a song by Bob Dylan, was most famously covered by The Jimi Hendrix Experience (*Electric Ladyland*, Polydor, 1968).

Robert Nesbitt, interviewed by the author, 2014.

HIDDEN TRACK: 'PLAY NASTY FOR ME'

The initials RSA stand for Royal New Zealand Returned and Services' Association, often referred to as the Returned Services' Association but best known simply as the RSA.

'Ten Guitars'. Composed by British entrepreneur Gordon Mills, this song first appeared on the B-side of 'Release Me' (Decca, 1967), a single by his protégé, the singer Engelbert Humperdinck, but became a New Zealand hit in its own right, and remains a staple of singalongs and showband repertoires.

'Help!' This song was composed by John Lennon and Paul McCartney and recorded by The Beatles (Parlophone, 1965) as the theme tune for the film of the same name.

'Desolation Row' is the closing song on Bob Dylan's album *Highway 61 Revisited* (Columbia, 1965), a surreal ten-verse ballad that incorporates such figures from history and literature as Cinderella, Casanova, Ophelia, Einstein (disguised as Robin Hood), Ezra Pound,

T.S. Eliot and the hunchback of Notre Dame.

Dick Dale is an American guitarist and pioneer of the surf rock style, utilising Eastern scales and heavy reverberation.

Buffalo Springfield was a seminal American folk-rock band in the mid to late 1960s, and included future superstars Neil Young and Stephen Stills.

Prog-rock is short for progressive rock, a genre developed in the late '60s and early '70s by groups such as Pink Floyd, The Moody Blues, Yes and King Crimson; they wrote, performed and recorded suites and long-form compositions, borrowing some of the structural and compositional conventions of classical music.

Frank Zappa and his group The Mothers of Invention created elaborate musical collages that referenced Dadaism and absurdism. An example is 'Brown Shoes Don't Make It', Zappa's self-described 'underground oratorio' from the Mothers' album *Absolutely Free* (Verve, 1967). The song shifts abruptly from doo-wop to vaudeville to what sound like television jingles, from orchestral fanfares to *musique concrète* to moments of aural anarchy, all in seven and a half minutes.

The Beatles' 'Happiness is a Warm Gun' from their album *The Beatles* (Apple, 1968) begins as a fingerpicked folk song in a minor key, briefly lumbers into waltz time, and skates across 9/4 for a few desperate bars before landing on a classic '50s doo-wop progression – the same chords as 'Earth Angel' and a thousand other vintage rock 'n' roll songs – which it repeats to its conclusion. The whole thing lasts about as long as 'A Hard Day's Night'. It is like a whole side of *The Beatles* compressed into a single song.

EVANGELISTS

Rick Bryant, unpublished memoir.

'The older generation … of the young': *Evening Post*, April 15, 1970.

'A programme note by organisers Riddell and Jones …

fantasamgorical hugglemaflop' – from programme for *Second National Blues Convention*, 1969.

Salient and *Craccum*, 1964–1974.

Rick Bryant, interviewed by the author, 2014.

Mark Bracefield, *An Administration Handbook For Universities Arts Festival*: Otago Universities Students Association, 1970.

'Unlike previous Arts … entertainment value': *Craccum*, July 9, 1968.

'Complaining in his opening paragraph … derivative and deficient': *Craccum*, September 2, 1968.

'I NEED YOU … Arts Festival and I need you': *Salient*, May 27, 1970.

PETER F. AND THE LIGHTS

When the *Highway* album was reissued in 2011, the first time on CD, these liner notes were mysteriously modified. A few names such as Gary the hassler and Steve the roadie had survived, some new ones (Lorraine and Helen) had been added, others had vanished. And someone had evidently decided to add thanks to God.

Peter Frater, interviewed by the author, 2015.

Chris Prowse, interviewed by the author, 2015.

INCREASING SOPHISTICATION

Tim Mulcare, *The Political Economy of Six O'Clock Closing*: New Zealand Institute for the Study of Competition and Regulation, 1999.

'Prime Minister Keith Holyoake … the gaiety and increasing sophistication of our city': *Evening Post*, February 5, 1972.

GLAM ROCK AND FANTASMAGORICAL HUGGLEMAFLOPS

The *New Faces*' clip of Space Waltz's 1974 performances and some of the judges' responses can be found on YouTube. In 1973, the year before Space Waltz hit the screens, Split Ends had tried the same thing, although their twisted vaudeville was trumped by the less threatening novelty of the Bulldogs Allstar Goodtime Band. In 1972 Shona Laing and John Hanlon had launched successful careers with *New Faces* appearances, riding the international singer-songwriter trend that had made household names out of the likes of Melanie and Cat Stevens.

Alastair Riddell, interviewed by the author, 2015.

Bluebottle was a character performed by Peter Sellers in the British radio comedy *The Goons*.

Rick Bryant, interviewed by the author, 2014.

'It looks like another one of those visiting rock concerts … looking up for the local music scene at last': *Hot Licks*, 1975.

A DRAGON'S TALE

Ray Goodwin, correspondence with author, 2014.

Details of recording 'Education' from Robert Taylor in interview with Nick Bollinger for Radio New Zealand, 2000.

'We discovered the meaning of his name … without any sign of repayment': *Hot Licks*, 1974.

Details and quotes from interview with Robert Taylor by the author for Radio New Zealand, 2000.

DEPARTURES

Greil Marcus, *Mystery Train: Images of America in Rock 'n' Roll Music*, fifth edition: Plume, New York, 1997. First published in 1975, this book was seminal in the development of rock literature. In a series of loosely interlinked essays on half a dozen American acts, from long-deceased bluesman Robert Johnson to then living Elvis Presley, Marcus made an argument for the study of rock 'n' roll as a way to understand American culture.

THE WINDY CITY STRUGGLERS GO ELECTRIC

Rick Bryant, interviewed by the author, 2014.

Jarrod Gilbert, *Patched: The History of Gangs in New Zealand*: Auckland University Press, 2013.

BROADER THEATRE

Rod Bryant, interviewed by the author, 2014.

MEDLEY: 'LAWDY MISS CLAWDY'/'SUNSHINE'

'It wasn't cut in a commercial studio ... raw and exciting.' Details about the recording of Johnny Devlin's 'Lawdy Miss Clawdy' largely come from Chris Bourke in *Blue Smoke*: Auckland University Press, 2010. Johnny Devlin cut two versions of the song six months apart. Although the first version sold reasonably well it received limited airplay: the New Zealand Broadcasting Service argued that the recording quality was not good enough. A faster and more popular version was cut with The Devils at Stebbing Recording Studios in time for Johnny's national tour over the summer of 1958–59.

'He had a rock 'n' roll suit made ... leather's out.' Interview with Johnny Devlin at Museum of Applied Arts and Sciences, Sydney, 2014, available on YouTube.

'NOT THE MUSICAL GENIUS BUSINESS'

'Hands ... mutton hams',Warren Barton: *Dominion*, July 30, 1997.

' ... like twin kilos of corned silverside', Alex Veysey: *Evening Post*, January 24, 1991.

'... one of life's great gargantuan, Rabelaisian characters', Alan Smythe, in Bernadette Rae, 'The Party's Over': *Weekend Magazine*, August 1997.

'He had been lured back to New Zealand ... and formed the Quincys', details from Gary Steel, *The Quincy Conserve Profile*:

AudioCulture, www.audioculture.co.nz

Jackie Matthews, interview with the author, 2014.

'There has been a tendency for musicians to play for themselves … we're in the entertainment business,' *New Zealand Herald*, March 27, 1973.

'Holden would also go to London to audition prospects … they lowered their asking price', details from Mark Scott, 'Selling the Track': *New Zealand Listener*, January 14, 1989.

Paul Davies, interviewed by the author, 2014.

'As well as providing our younger patrons with the best musical entertainment … employment with their musical commitments': *Brewnews*, August 1974.

Mike Corless, interviewed by the author, 2014.

PIG'S HEAD AND PIPI BOLOGNESE

'During Labour's brief government, between 1972 and 1975 … a possible antidote to the ills of modern society, as well as a means of showing people the virtues of a simpler life', Margaret Hayward, *Diary of the Kirk Years*: Cape Catley/Reed, 1981.

SHOWDOWN AT THE SPECTRUM BAR

Clinton Brown, interviewed by the author, 2015.

PUNKS AND INDEPENDENTS

Charley Gray, interviewed by the author, 2014.

'… against consistent opposition from a powerful lobby that included Alcoholics Anonymous, the Salvation Army and the breweries – a handful of high-end restaurants had finally been granted licences to serve wine and beer.' Some details from Conrad Bollinger, *Grog's Own Country: The Story of Liquor Licensing in New Zealand*: Minerva, Auckland, 1967.

TRENDY LEFTIES AND ORDINARY BLOKES

How to Murder Your Wife: Television New Zealand/Screentime, 2015.

James K. Baxter, *A Death Song for Mr Mouldybroke*: Caxton Press, 1967. First printed in *New Zealand Monthly Review*, November, 1967.

Some details about the life of Norman Kirk from David Grant, *The Mighty Totara: The Life and Times of Norman Kirk*: Random House, Auckland, 2014.

Some details about the life of Robert Muldoon from Barry Gustafson, *His Way: A Biography of Robert Muldoon*: Auckland University Press, 2000.

ON THE STREET

'When it comes to a decision … I would be failing in my duty if I did not accept the criticism and do what I believed to be right', Margaret Hayward, *Diary of the Kirk Years*: Cape Catley/Reed, 1981.

EPILOGUE

Robert Nesbitt, interviewed by the author, 2014.

Rick Bryant, interviewed by the author, 2014.

'Richard Holden was promoted … thanking everyone for coming', details from Catherine Woulfe, 'Funeral for a Colourful Character': *Sunday Star-Times*, August 31, 2008.

'Entertainer Tony Bee will do anything for a laugh … and the people friendly', based on press releases from Lion Breweries' archives.

Janet Clouston, interviewed by the author, 2015.

Photographs and images

Index